20-MINUTE MEDITERRANEAN AIR FRYER COOKBOOK

Revolutionize Your Diet with 2000 Days of Irresistible, Easy-to-Make Air Fryer Recipes to Cut Cooking Time but not Flavor

Sandrine Kelly

Table of Contents

HERE IS YOUR BONUS!

"Air Fryer Cooking Time and Temperature Charts"

Your Essential Printable Guide to Perfect Air Fryer Cooking Every Time

Inside you will find:

- Cooking Temperatures

- Estimated Air Fryer Cooking Times Range

- Essential Notes for Every Kind of Foods

- Accurate Directions to Reach the Safe Target Internal Temperature for Poultry, Beef, and Pork

SCAN HERE TO DOWNLOAD IT

SCAN HERE!

AIR FRYER
COOKING TIME
AND TEMPERATURE
CHARTS

Perfect Your Cooking Techniques
through a Complete Guide to Cooking
Times and Temperatures for Various
Ingredients in the Air Fryer

BONUS EXTRA

Sandrine Kelly

Introduction

The Fusion of Air Frying and Mediterranean Diet

The culinary world is constantly evolving, merging traditional practices with modern innovations. At the forefront of this evolution is the fusion of the Mediterranean diet, a time-honored tradition, with the contemporary method of air frying. This combination is not just a mere culinary experiment; it represents a significant step forward in how we approach cooking and nutrition.

The Mediterranean diet, with its origins rooted in the sun-kissed regions of Southern Europe, is known for its emphasis on fresh, nutritious ingredients. Characterized by an abundant use of vegetables, fruits, whole grains, nuts, and olive oil, it stands as a paragon of healthy eating. Integral to this diet is the consumption of seafood and a moderate intake of dairy and poultry, with red meat and sweets enjoyed on a less frequent basis. This dietary pattern, lauded for its health benefits, encapsulates the essence of simplicity and natural flavors.

Enter air frying, a modern cooking technique that has transformed our perception of 'fried' foods. An air fryer operates by circulating hot air around food, creating a crispy layer akin to traditional frying but with significantly less oil. This method not only reduces the overall calorie and fat content but also preserves the nutritional integrity of the ingredients. Air frying's ability to deliver a healthier alternative to conventional frying aligns seamlessly with the core principles of the Mediterranean diet.

The fusion of these two distinct culinary approaches offers a multitude of benefits. For starters, it provides a healthier way to enjoy fried foods without veering away from the Mediterranean diet's focus on nutrition. Vegetables cooked in an air fryer retain their color, texture, and nutrients, while proteins like fish and chicken are prepared with minimal oil, keeping them light and heart-healthy. This method of cooking not only complements the nutritional profile of Mediterranean ingredients but also intensifies their natural flavors.

Moreover, air frying caters to the modern fast-paced lifestyle without compromising on the quality of meals. It offers a quick, convenient, and clean way to prepare food, fitting perfectly into the busy schedules of today's households. This ease of use encourages more people to try Mediterranean recipes, which they might have otherwise found too time-consuming or complex to prepare.

Furthermore, this fusion is an invitation to culinary creativity. Traditional Mediterranean recipes can be adapted and transformed, offering a new dimension of texture and flavor. Imagine crispy falafel, tender yet crunchy vegetables, or lightly golden seafood, all prepared with minimal oil and maximum taste. The versatility of air frying opens up a world of possibilities, enabling home cooks to experiment and innovate while staying true to the healthy foundations of the Mediterranean diet.

In essence, the fusion of air frying and the Mediterranean diet is a celebration of healthy, flavorful eating. It bridges the gap between traditional culinary wisdom and modern cooking technology, offering a practical and enjoyable way to eat well. As we delve deeper into this fusion, we uncover not just a collection of recipes but a lifestyle choice — one that cherishes good food, good health, and the joy of eating.

Chapter 1

The Essence of Mediterranean Cooking

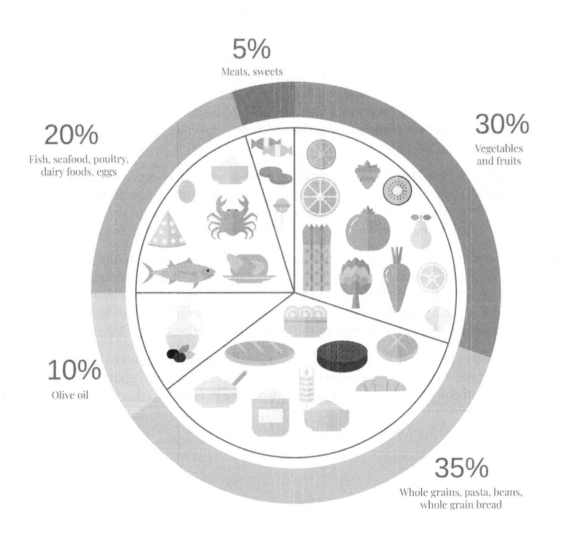

5%
Meats, sweets

30%
Vegetables
and fruits

20%
Fish, seafood, poultry,
dairy foods, eggs

10%
Olive oil

35%
Whole grains, pasta, beans,
whole grain bread

In the realm of culinary traditions, few are as revered and time-honored as the Mediterranean diet. This diet, a tapestry of the rich cultural heritage of countries like Italy, Greece, and Spain, is more than a mere eating plan; it's a testament to a lifestyle that values health, freshness, and the unadulterated flavors of nature.

It isn't just about individual foods; it's a holistic approach to eating and living. It emphasizes natural ingredients, simple cooking methods, and enjoying meals with others.

This diet is renowned for its health benefits, including heart health, weight management, and overall wellness.

The Mediterranean diet is a celebration of whole foods. This means an emphasis on ingredients in their natural, unprocessed form. Vegetables, whole grains, fruits, nuts, seeds, and legumes are not just components of a meal; they are the stars. These foods are not only abundant in essential nutrients but also in flavors, colors, and textures that delight the senses. When you indulge in a Mediterranean meal, you're experiencing a bounty of the earth, a feast that is as nourishing to the body as it is pleasing to the palate.

Another cornerstone of the Mediterranean diet is its use of healthy fats. Unlike diets that shun fat, the Mediterranean diet embraces it, but wisely. The principal source of fat is olive oil, the liquid gold of the Mediterranean. Rich in monounsaturated fatty acids, it is heart-friendly and brings a distinct flavor to dishes. The diet also includes fatty fish, such as mackerel and salmon, which are rich in omega-3 fatty acids known for their cardiovascular and cognitive benefits. This conscious choice of fats aligns with modern nutritional guidelines that recognize the value of healthy fats in our diet.

What actually distinguishes the Mediterranean diet is its emphasis on freshness. The diet is rooted in the seasons, meaning that meals are often dictated by what is available locally and ripe. This not only ensures a diet that is varied and nutrient-rich but also one that is environmentally sustainable. Fresh herbs, like basil, oregano, and rosemary, play a crucial role, adding aroma and depth to recipes without the addiction of salt or fat.

As we integrate air frying into Mediterranean cooking, these principles guide our approach. Air frying, known for its ability to 'fry' food with a fraction of the oil typically used, aligns perfectly with the diet's emphasis on health and natural flavors. Vegetables air-fried retain their nutritional integrity and gain a delightful crispness. Meats and fish are cooked to perfection, capturing their natural juiciness without the need for excess oil.

This fusion is a harmonic marriage of tradition and technology, not just a culinary innovation. It offers a way to enjoy the wholesome goodness of the Mediterranean diet with the convenience and health benefits of air frying.

Let's summarize the key components of the Mediterranean Diet:

- **Fresh Vegetables and Fruits:** Packed with vitamins, minerals, and fiber, they're essential for a balanced diet.
    - Examples: Leafy greens, tomatoes, cucumbers, oranges, apples.

- **Whole Grains:** Whole grains are consumed regularly, providing essential nutrients and fiber.
    - Examples: Whole wheat bread, brown rice, quinoa, barley.

- **Nuts and Legumes:** These provide protein, healthy fats, and fiber.
    - Examples: Almonds, lentils, chickpeas, beans.

- **Olive Oil:** A primary source of healthy fat, olive oil is used instead of butter or other saturated fats.
    - Benefits: Rich in monounsaturated fats, good for heart health.

- **Seafood:** Fish and shellfish are key for their omega-3 fatty acids.
    - Examples: Salmon, trout, mussels, shrimp.

- **Moderate Dairy:** Dairy is consumed in moderation, often as cheese and yogurt.
    - Benefits: Provides calcium and protein.

- **Limited Red Meat:** Red meat is eaten less frequently, focusing on leaner proteins.
    - Suggestion: Opt for poultry, fish, or plant-based proteins instead.

- **Wine in Moderation:** Often included in meals but consumed in moderate amounts.

- **Physical Activity:** Regular exercise complements the diet for overall health.

Adapting Mediterranean Recipes for Air Frying

The fusion of air frying technology with the Mediterranean diet is a culinary innovation that marries health with convenience. This marriage, however, calls for a thoughtful adaptation of traditional Mediterranean recipes to suit the air fryer's unique cooking method. To master this fusion, one must understand both the subtleties of Mediterranean cuisine and the technicalities of air frying, ensuring that the essence of these time-honored recipes is preserved while reaping the benefits of modern cooking technology.

Firstly, consider the cornerstone of Mediterranean cooking: vegetables. When adapting vegetable-based dishes for the air fryer, it is crucial to cut them uniformly to ensure even cooking. Vegetables like bell peppers, zucchini, eggplants, and tomatoes, staples in Mediterranean cuisine, benefit from a light toss in olive oil and a sprinkle of herbs before air frying. This not only retains their natural moisture but also enhances their flavors. The air fryer's rapid air circulation crisps these vegetables beautifully, mimicking the effects of traditional grilling or roasting.

For Mediterranean seafood dishes, the air fryer offers a perfect platform for cooking delicate items like fish fillets, shrimp, and calamari. The key is to not overcrowd the air fryer basket, allowing for efficient air circulation. A light brush of olive oil and a seasoning of fresh herbs, garlic, and lemon can elevate the natural flavors of seafood, which the air fryer locks in, delivering a result that is crispy on the outside and succulently moist on the inside.

Adapting poultry and meat recipes requires attention to marination and cooking time. Mediterranean cuisine often involves marinating meats in olive oil, lemon juice, and an array of herbs and spices. This marination is crucial in air frying, as it imparts deep flavors and tenderizes the meat. It is important to note that cooking times in an air fryer may be shorter than traditional methods, so monitoring the cooking process is vital to avoid overcooking.

Another aspect to consider is the moisture content in fresh vegetables and meats. The quick air circulation technique of the air fryer can occasionally result in drier textures.. To counter this, slight modifications, such as marinating meats or lightly coating vegetables in oil mixed with herbs, can help retain moisture and enhance flavors. Furthermore, ingredients that typically require longer cooking times, such as whole potatoes or large cuts of meat, might need to be pre-cooked or cut into smaller pieces to ensure even cooking in the air fryer.

Adjustments in cooking temperatures is also paramount in successfully adapting Mediterranean recipes for the air fryer. Food is often cooked at a higher intensity with air fryers. Recipes that call for slow cooking at low temperatures in conventional methods may require a lower temperature setting in an air fryer but for a shorter duration. It's about finding the right balance between temperature and time to replicate the texture and flavor of the original dish as closely as possible.

Using a food thermometer can be particularly helpful in ensuring meats and seafood are cooked to the right temperature without drying out.

In addition, the layering of ingredients in the air fryer basket needs consideration. Unlike conventional cooking methods where ingredients can be cooked in larger quantities, the air fryer works best when food is cooked in single layers or smaller batches. This ensures even cooking and crisping, which is particularly important for recipes like vegetable gratins or layered casseroles, common in Mediterranean cuisine.

Lastly, the essence of Mediterranean cooking is simplicity and allowing ingredients' inherent tastes to show. This principle should guide the adaptation process. The air fryer should be seen as a tool to enhance these flavors, not overpower them. By understanding the strengths of the air fryer – its ability to cook quickly, evenly, and with less oil – traditional Mediterranean recipes can be transformed into healthier, yet equally delicious versions of themselves.

Chapter 2

Air Fryer Basics

Introduction to Air Frying: A Healthful Approach to Culinary Innovation

The artistry of culinary preparation has always held a cherished spot in the heart of the families. As tradition marries innovation, we find ourselves on the cusp of a healthful cooking revolution with the advent of the air fryer. This remarkable appliance, often considered as a healthier alternative to conventional frying, allows for the recreation of our favorite crispy delights sans the excessive oil.

The crux of the air fryer lies in its ability to circulate hot air at a high speed which crisps up the food items to a desirable golden perfection. This is a far cry from the traditional deep frying methods which dunk food items in copious amounts of oil. The sheer reduction in oil usage translates to lower calorie and fat content, a blessing for those desiring a healthier lifestyle without bidding adieu to their beloved fried foods.

But it isn't merely about less oil. The air fryer brings to the table a remarkably reduced cooking time. In the modern whirlpool of hectic schedules, the allure of a quicker meal preparation is undeniably enticing. The efficiency of the air fryer encapsulates the modern-day necessity for speed and convenience, all without undermining the essence of a wholesome meal.

Moreover, air fryers offer a simplified user interface. With straightforward settings, one can effortlessly create a smoother pathway into the world of health-conscious cooking. The air fryer, with its compact design, also lends itself to a neat kitchen setup, an aesthetic appeal that resonates with contemporary homemakers.

What makes the air fryer an epitome of culinary innovation is its versatility. Its capabilities extend beyond mere frying; it graciously accommodates grilling, roasting, and baking, becoming an indomitable workhorse in the kitchen. This versatility invokes a creative spark, allowing one to explore an array of culinary endeavors. The marriage between health and taste that the air fryer manifests is a testament to the evolution of modern-day cooking apparatus, pushing the boundaries of what is possible in the domestic culinary sphere.

Choosing the Right Air Fryer

Selecting an air fryer that best suits your individual needs requires considering several critical factors: size, capacity, features, price, and brand. Each of these elements plays a significant role in determining the suitability of an air fryer for your kitchen and lifestyle.

Firstly, **size** is a crucial consideration. Air fryers are available in a variety of sizes, from compact models ideal for small families or individuals to larger units designed for cooking bigger meals. When assessing size, consider not only the amount of food you plan to cook regularly but also the counter space available in your kitchen. A smaller air fryer may be sufficient for quick meals or side dishes, while a larger one might be necessary for complete family meals or entertaining guests.

Capacity closely ties with size but deserves its own consideration. It refers to how much food an air fryer can cook at once. Capacities can vary from as little as 2 quarts to more than 6 quarts. Smaller units are ideal for singles or couples, whereas larger families or those who often host gatherings might find a larger capacity more practical. It's important to note that a larger capacity might also mean a bigger overall footprint of the appliance, so balance the need for cooking volume with the space available.

Next, examine the **features** offered by different air fryers. Modern air fryers come equipped with a range of functionalities, from basic temperature and time controls to advanced presets for specific foods. Some models offer additional features like dehydration, baking, grilling, and even rotisserie functions. Consider what types of foods you plan to cook and select a model with features that align with your culinary aspirations. Features like digital displays, easy-to-clean surfaces, and dishwasher-safe components can also add to the convenience.

Price is another significant factor in selecting an air fryer. Air fryers are available at a wide range of price points, often reflecting their size, capacity, and feature set. It's essential to set a realistic budget and find a balance between affordability and the quality or features you desire. Cheaper models might offer basic functionality, which could be sufficient for your needs. However, investing in a higher-priced model could provide long-term value with more robust build quality and advanced features.

Finally, **brand** reputation and reviews can guide your decision. Established brands often offer reliability and customer support, which can be invaluable for first-time users. Customer evaluations and ratings can provide information about the durability and performance of various models. Look for reviews that specifically address the aspects you care about, such as ease of use, cleaning, and the quality of the food produced.

Comparison of different types of air fryers

Predominantly, air fryers fall into three categories: basket-style, oven-style, and multifunctional models. Understanding the nuances of each type is key to making an informed decision that aligns with your culinary needs and preferences.

Basket-style air fryers are perhaps the most common and widely recognized type. Characterized by their compact design, these models feature a removable basket where food is placed for cooking. The primary advantage of basket-style air fryers lies in their simplicity and ease of use. They usually take up less counter space, making them perfect for smaller kitchens or for those who prioritize convenience and space efficiency. These models are perfect for everyday tasks like frying chicken, cooking frozen foods, or roasting vegetables. However, their smaller cooking capacity may not be suitable for larger families or for preparing multiple dishes simultaneously.

In contrast, **oven-style air fryers** offer a larger cooking space and often resemble a miniature conventional oven. They usually come with multiple racks or trays, allowing different foods to be cooked at the same time. This feature makes oven-style air fryers a preferable option for larger households or for those who often entertain guests. Additionally, these models tend to offer more versatility, as they can often function as a mini-oven, suitable for baking, toasting, and even dehydrating. The trade-off, however, is their larger size, which requires more counter space and storage.

Multifunctional air fryers represent the latest evolution in air frying technology, combining the features of both basket-style and oven-style models with additional cooking functions. These units are designed to serve as an all-in-one kitchen appliance, capable of air frying, baking, grilling, and sometimes even pressure cooking or slow cooking. Multifunctional models are ideal for those looking to consolidate kitchen appliances and for avid cooks who value versatility. They allow for a wide range of culinary experiments and can handle everything from air frying and roasting to baking cakes and preparing stews. The downside is that these models can be quite bulky and may come with a higher price tag. Additionally, the multitude of functions can sometimes mean a compromise in the performance of individual features compared to specialized units.

When comparing these types, consider your cooking habits, the volume of food you typically prepare, and the available space in your kitchen. Basket-style air fryers are a great entry point for those new to air frying, offering simplicity and compactness. Oven-style models are suited for those who need more cooking capacity and enjoy preparing multiple dishes at once. Multifunctional air fryers are the go-to for culinary enthusiasts who desire a range of cooking methods in one appliance.

In conclusion, choosing the right air fryer is a personal decision that should be guided by a clear understanding of your cooking habits, kitchen space, desired features, budget, and the credibility of the brand. By evaluating each of these aspects, you may choose an air fryer that satisfies your culinary needs and improves your cooking experience, allowing you to fully embrace the convenience and versatility of air frying.

Essential Accessories and Equipment

1. **Air Fryer Baskets**:
   - **Purpose**: The primary container where food is placed for cooking.
   - **Importance**: Essential for even air circulation and consistent cooking.

2. **Racks and Skewers**:
   - **Racks**: Allow for layering of food, maximizing cooking space.
   - **Skewers**: Ideal for making kebabs and ensuring even cooking of items like meat, vegetables, or seafood.

3. **Oil Sprayers**:
   - **Function**: Enables you to apply a fine mist of oil, ensuring light and even coating.
   - **Benefits**: Helps achieve crispiness with minimal oil use, aligning with healthier cooking goals.

4. **Thermometers**:
   - **Types**: Digital and analog options to suit preferences.
   - **Usage**: Critical for ensuring food, especially meats, are cooked to the correct internal temperature.

5. **Tongs and Spatulas**:
   - **Tongs**: Provide a safe way to handle and flip food items during cooking.
   - **Spatulas**: Useful for removing food from the basket, especially delicate items like vegetables or fish.

6. **Parchment Liners**:
   - **Design**: Often perforated to facilitate airflow.
   - **Advantage**: Simplifies cleanup and ensures that smaller food items do not fall through the basket.

7. **Baking Pans and Dishes**:
   - **Variety**: Available in specific sizes to fit within air fryer baskets.
   - **Use**: Ideal for dishes like casseroles, cakes, or quiches.

8. **Silicone Mats or Cups**:
   - **Function**: Provide a non-stick surface for baking or roasting.
   - **Flexibility**: Can be used for making muffins, small cakes, or egg bites.

9. **Brushes for Marinades or Oil**:
   - **Usage**: For applying marinades or oil to food pre-cooking.
   - **Type**: Silicone brushes are preferred for their durability and ease of cleaning.

10. **Gloves or Oven Mitts**:
    - **Purpose**: To protect hands from high temperatures when handling the air fryer basket.
    - **Material**: Heat-resistant materials are recommended.

11. **Storage Solutions**:
    - **Options**: Racks or holders for organizing and storing accessories.
    - **Benefit**: Keeps accessories easily accessible and kitchen counters uncluttered.

12. **Cleaning Tools**:
    - **Necessity**: Brushes and sponges specifically designed for cleaning air fryer baskets and accessories.
    - **Importance**: Regular cleaning extends the life of the air fryer and maintains performance.

Setting Up Your Air Fryer

Setting up your air fryer for the first time is a crucial step to ensure its optimal functioning and longevity. Here's a detailed step-by-step guide to help you get started:

1. **Unboxing and Inspection:**
   - Carefully remove the air fryer from its packaging.
   - Inspect for any visible damage or missing parts.
   - Ensure all packaging materials are removed from the air fryer.

2. **Choosing the Location:**
   - Place the air fryer on a flat, stable surface.
   - Ensure there's ample space around it, typically a few inches, for proper air circulation.

3. **Assembly:**
   - Assemble any detachable parts like the basket or tray as per the manufacturer's instructions.
   - Ensure all components are securely fitted.

4. **Initial Cleaning:**
   - Wash the removable components (basket, tray, etc.) with warm soapy water.
   - Wipe down the outside and inside of the air fryer with a moist towel.
   - Ensure all parts are dry before reassembling.

5. **First-Time Heating:**
   - Plug in the air fryer and turn it on.
   - Set it to a moderate temperature (usually around 350°F or 180°C) and run it empty for about 10-15 minutes.
   - This procedure aids in the removal of any remaining odors or manufacturing oils.

6. **Familiarizing with Controls:**
   - Review the control panel and settings.
   - Understand basic functions like temperature and time adjustments, start/stop, and any preset programs.

7. **Safety Precautions:**
   - Familiarize yourself with safety features and instructions.
   - Understand the correct way to insert and remove the basket to prevent burns or spills.

8. **Reading the Manual:**
   - Thoroughly read the user manual for specific instructions and safety warnings.
   - Note any special recommendations from the manufacturer regarding the use and maintenance of the air fryer.

9. **Testing with Simple Recipes:**
   - Start with simple recipes to get a feel for cooking times and temperature settings.
   - Observe how the air fryer cooks and adjust settings as necessary for future use.

10. **Ongoing Maintenance:**
   - After each use, clean the air fryer to prevent build-up of food residues.
   - Regularly check for any wear or damage to ensure safe operation.

Setting up your air fryer properly is the first step to a delightful and efficient cooking experience. By following these steps, you can ensure your air fryer is ready to deliver delicious and healthy meals. Remember, Each air fryer model may have its own set of instructions, so always consult the manufacturer's manual for specifics.

Basic Controls and Settings

Preheating the Air Fryer

Preheating your air fryer is a step often overlooked, yet it is crucial for certain recipes. Preheating the air fryer guarantees that it reaches the desired cooking temperature before you add your food. This is particularly important for achieving a crispy exterior on foods like French fries, chicken wings, or vegetables. To preheat, simply turn on your air fryer and set it to the required temperature for a few minutes, usually around three to five, depending on the model. Some air fryers come with a preheat button, making this process even easier. Remember, not all recipes require preheating, so refer to your specific recipe for guidance.

Understanding Basic Controls

Air fryers typically come with a range of controls that allow you to set the cooking temperature and time. These controls can be dials or digital touchpads, depending on your model. The temperature control is crucial for cooking your food correctly. Most air fryers can reach temperatures up to 400°F (200°C), allowing for a variety of cooking techniques from frying and baking, to roasting.

The timer control, often going up to 30 or 60 minutes, helps you set the duration of cooking. It's important to note that cooking times can vary based on the type of food, its volume, and your desired level of doneness. Many air fryers will automatically shut off once the timer ends, which is a helpful safety feature.

Settings and Features

Modern air fryers come with a variety of settings and features designed to make cooking easier. Familiarize yourself with these to fully utilize your air fryer:

1. **Temperature and Time Adjustments**: The basic function of any air fryer, allowing you to set the cooking temperature and duration as per your recipe.

2. **Preset Programs**: Many air fryers come with preset programs for common foods like chicken, fish, steak, or vegetables. These presets are programmed with recommended cooking times and temperatures for specific foods, simplifying the cooking process.

3. **Pause and Shake/Flip Feature**: Some models allow you to pause the cooking process to shake or flip the food for even cooking. This feature is particularly useful for items like French fries or vegetables that need to be tossed during cooking.

4. **Keep Warm Function**: This feature keeps your food warm after cooking without overcooking it.

Maintenance and Care

Understanding how to care for your air fryer is just as important as knowing how to use it. Regular cleaning is required to keep its longevity and performance. Most air fryers have dishwasher safe removable trays and baskets, making cleanup easy. Wipe down the exterior and the main unit with a damp cloth to keep it clean.

Cooking Various Food Types

When embarking on the culinary adventure of air frying, understanding how to adeptly cook various food types is paramount. The air fryer, a versatile and innovative appliance, allows you to explore a wide range of dishes, from succulent meats to crispy vegetables, convenient frozen foods, and even delectable baked goods. Each category, however, demands specific considerations to ensure the best results.

Air Frying Meats

Cooking meats in an air fryer is a healthier option than standard frying methods because it uses less fat and oil yet maintaining delicious flavor and texture. To achieve the perfect doneness and a desirable crust:

- **Preheat** the air fryer before adding the meat. This ensures a crisp exterior.

- **Season** your meat generously. Air frying enhances flavors, making spices and herbs more pronounced.

- **Avoid overcrowding** the basket to ensure even cooking. Cook in batches if necessary.

- **Use a meat thermometer** to check for doneness, especially for larger cuts of meat or poultry.

- **Let the meat rest** for a few minutes after cooking. This redistributes the liquids, resulting in a moist and tasty dish.

Air Frying Vegetables

Air frying transforms vegetables into a tantalizing experience, offering a great way to enjoy your greens:

- **Cut vegetables into uniform sizes** for even cooking.

- **Lightly coat with oil**. A small amount of oil helps to crisp the vegetables and enhance their natural flavors.

- **Season as desired**, and don't hesitate to experiment with different herbs and spices.

- **Shake the basket occasionally** during cooking to promote even browning and crispness.

Air Frying Frozen Foods

One of the air fryer's charms is its ability to cook frozen foods efficiently, delivering a result that's often superior to traditional oven-baking:

- **No need to thaw**. Most frozen foods can be cooked directly from the freezer, adding convenience.

- **Adjust the cooking time and temperature**. Generally, frozen foods require a slightly longer cooking time than their fresh counterparts.

- **Shake or flip halfway through** the cooking time to ensure even cooking.

Air Frying Baked Goods

The air fryer is not just for savory dishes; it's also adept at baking. From muffins to cakes, the air fryer provides a unique way to bake:

- **Use air fryer-safe baking dishes** or molds. Ensure they fit comfortably in the basket.

- **Reduce the temperature**. Air fryers typically require a lower temperature than conventional ovens for baking.

- **Monitor closely**, as baked goods can cook faster in an air fryer than in an oven.

Additional Tips

- **Prevent sticking** by either lightly oiling the basket or using parchment liners with holes.

- **Avoid smoke** by placing a small amount of water in the drawer beneath the basket when cooking fatty foods.

- **Clean regularly**. Ensure the air fryer is clean before each use for optimal performance and taste.

Maintenance and Cleaning

Maintaining and cleaning your air fryer is an essential aspect of its care, crucial for ensuring both the longevity and optimal performance of the appliance. Regular maintenance not only extends the life of your air fryer but also guarantees that it operates efficiently and safely, contributing to the consistent quality of your culinary creations. In this comprehensive guide, we will explore effective and safe methods to clean various components of the air fryer, ensuring it remains a reliable tool in your kitchen.

To begin with, regular maintenance of your air fryer is not labor-intensive but it is certainly necessary. After each use, it's important to clean the air fryer to prevent build-up of food particles and grease, which can affect its performance and potentially pose a fire hazard. Moreover, lingering odors and flavors can be transferred to other foods cooked later. Therefore, a routine cleanup after every cooking session is recommended.

Cleaning the Air Fryer Basket and Pan

The basket and pan are where most of the cooking action happens, and as such, they are prone to the most residue build-up. Most air fryer pans and baskets are dishwasher safe and non-stick, making cleanup a breeze. If you're washing by hand, let them soak in warm, soapy water for about 10 minutes before cleaning. Use a non-abrasive sponge or cloth to avoid damaging the non-stick coating. For stubborn residue, you can use baking soda as a mild abrasive. Ensure they are completely dry before reinserting into the air fryer.

Cleaning the Interior of the Air Fryer

The interior of the air fryer, although not in direct contact with food, can accumulate grease and residue over time. To clean, first ensure the appliance is unplugged and completely cool. Wipe down the interior with a damp cloth or sponge. Harsh chemical cleaners and abrasive sponges should be avoided as they can damage the interior surface. For hard-to-reach areas, a soft-bristled brush can be helpful.

Cleaning the Heating Element

Over time, the heating element can accumulate grease and food particles, which can affect its efficiency. To clean the heating element, turn the appliance upside down for easier access. Brush away any residue with a soft-bristled brush. You can also use a damp cloth, but ensure that no water gets into the electrical components.

Exterior Maintenance

The exterior of your air fryer can be wiped down with a damp cloth. If there are fingerprints or other marks on a stainless-steel surface, a bit of glass cleaner on a microfiber cloth can work wonders. It's important to keep the exterior clean not just for aesthetic reasons but also to maintain the appliance's functionality, as grime can interfere with the controls.

NOTE: Never clean the air fryer while it's still hot, as this can lead to burns or damage to the appliance.

Troubleshooting Common Issues

1. **Food Not Cooking Evenly:**

   - **Cause:** Overcrowding the basket or uneven placement of food.
   - **Solution:** Cook in smaller batches and arrange food in a single layer, ensuring space between items for better air circulation.

2. **Air Fryer Not Heating Up:**

   - **Cause:** Electrical issues, thermostat issues, or malfunctioning heating element.
   - **Solution:** Check the power connection, reset the air fryer if it has a reset function, and ensure the timer is set correctly. Consult the manufacturer or a professional technician if the problem persists.

3. **Excessive Smoke During Cooking:**

   - **Cause:** Accumulation of grease in the basket or using high-fat foods.
   - **Solution:** Clean the air fryer thoroughly after each use. When cooking high-fat foods, add a little water to the drawer beneath the basket to prevent grease from overheating.

4. **Unpleasant Odors:**

   - **Cause:** Residue from previous cooking sessions or new appliance smell.

- **Solution:** Clean the air fryer thoroughly. For new air fryer smell, run the empty air fryer at high temperature for a few minutes.

5. **Air Fryer Suddenly Stops Working:**
   - **Cause:** Overheating or tripped circuit breaker.
   - **Solution:** Allow the air fryer to cool down before restarting. Check your home's electrical panel to see if the circuit breaker needs resetting.

6. **Food Not Crisping Up:**
   - **Cause:** Insufficient oil or incorrect cooking temperature.
   - **Solution:** Lightly coat food with oil for a crispier texture. Ensure the air fryer is preheated and the temperature is set according to the recipe.

7. **White Smoke Coming From the Air Fryer:**
   - **Cause:** Burning of excess fat or food particles.
   - **Solution:** Add water to the drawer beneath the basket to minimize smoke. Clean the appliance thoroughly to remove residual fat.

8. **Control Panel Issues:**
   - **Cause:** Faulty touchpad or electrical issues.
   - **Solution:** Ensure the air fryer is plugged in correctly. If the touchpad is unresponsive, reset the air fryer or consult the manufacturer.

9. **Peeling Non-Stick Coating:**
   - **Cause:** Use of abrasive sponges or utensils.
   - **Solution:** Use soft sponges and non-metallic utensils to prevent damage to the non-stick coating.

10. **Difficulty Closing the Air Fryer Drawer:**
    - **Cause:** Overfilling or misalignment of the basket.
    - **Solution:** Avoid overfilling the basket. Check and adjust the basket to ensure it fits into the drawer properly.

Chapter 3

Breakfast Recipes

As you journey through this section, diving deep into recipes that evoke the essence of Mediterranean mornings, remember this isn't just about replicating a meal; it's about embracing a philosophy. A philosophy that cherishes freshness, celebrates simplicity, and above all, underscores the sheer joy of a meal had right. Welcome to the Mediterranean breakfast – where every dawn heralds a delectable discovery.

Air Fryer Mediterranean Frittata

Preparation Time: 10 minutes
Cooking Time: 15 minutes

Servings: 4

INGREDIENTS

- 6 eggs
- 1/4 cup milk
- 1 cup chopped spinach
- 1/2 cup halved cherry tomatoes
- 1/3 cup crumbled feta cheese
- 1/4 cup sliced Kalamata olives
- Salt and pepper, to taste
- Olive oil spray

INSTRUCTIONS

1. In a large bowl, whisk together eggs, milk, salt, and pepper.
2. Stir in spinach, cherry tomatoes, feta cheese, and Kalamata olives.
3. Preheat the air fryer to 360°F (182°C).
4. Coat the basket of the air fryer with olive oil spray.
5. Pour the egg mixture into the basket.
6. Cook for about 15 minutes or until the frittata is lightly golden.

Nutritional Value (per serving): Calories: 180, Fat: 13g, Carbohydrates: 3g, Protein: 12g

---

Air Fryer Greek Yogurt Pancakes

Preparation Time: 10 minutes
Cooking Time: 8 minutes

Servings: 2

INGREDIENTS

- 1 cup all-purpose flour
- 1/2 cup Greek yogurt
- 1 egg
- 1 tsp baking powder
- 1/2 tsp vanilla extract
- 2 tbsp honey
- Olive oil spray

INSTRUCTIONS

1. In a mixing bowl, combine flour and baking powder.
2. Mix Greek yogurt, vanilla extract, egg, and honey, in another bowl.
3. Combine the wet and dry ingredients until just mixed.
4. Preheat the air fryer to 350°F (177°C).
5. Form small pancakes and set them in the basket or on a greased air fryer tray.
6. Cook for about 4 minutes per side.
7. Serve with additional honey or toppings of choice.

Nutritional Value (per serving): Calories: 290, Fat: 4g, Carbohydrates: 53g, Protein: 12g

Air Fryer Mediterranean Breakfast Sandwich

Preparation Time: 5 minutes
Cooking Time: 10 minutes

Servings: 2

INGREDIENTS

- *2 whole grain English muffins*
- *2 eggs*
- *4 slices of tomato*

- *1/2 cup baby spinach leaves*
- *1/4 cup crumbled feta cheese*
- *Olive oil spray*

INSTRUCTIONS

1. Split the English muffins and place them in the air fryer.
2. Cook at 350°F (177°C) for 3 minutes until lightly toasted.
3. Remove the muffins and set aside.
4. Spray the air fryer basket with olive oil.
5. Crack the eggs into the basket, being careful to keep them separate.
6. Cook at 370°F (188°C) for about 5 minutes or until eggs are cooked.
7. Assemble the sandwiches by placing spinach leaves, a slice of tomato, an egg, and feta cheese on each muffin bottom. Top with the remaining muffin half.
8. Serve immediately.

Nutritional Value (per serving): Calories: 320, Fat: 15g, Carbohydrates: 28g, Protein: 18g

---

Air Fryer Olive & Tomato Shakshuka

Preparation Time: 10 minutes
Cooking Time: 15 minutes

Servings: 2

INGREDIENTS

- *4 eggs*
- *1 cup canned diced tomatoes*
- *1/4 cup sliced Kalamata olives*
- *1/4 cup diced onion*

- *1 minced garlic clove*
- *1/2 tsp cumin*
- *1/2 tsp paprika*
- *Olive oil*

INSTRUCTIONS

1. Preheat the air fryer to 350°F (177°C).
2. In a bowl, mix together diced tomatoes, Kalamata olives, onion, garlic, cumin, and paprika.
3. Coat the basket of the air fryer with olive oil.

4. Pour the tomato mixture into the basket and cook for 5 minutes.
5. Crack the eggs on top of the tomato mixture, spacing them evenly.
6. Cook for an additional 10 minutes or until the eggs are cooked.
7. Serve warm, spooning the tomato mixture and an egg onto plates.

Nutritional Value (per serving): Calories: 287, Fat: 21g, Carbohydrates: 12.5g, Protein: 13.8g

---

Air Fryer Mediterranean Veggie Omelette

Preparation Time: 5 minutes   **Servings:** 2
Cooking Time: 8 minutes

INGREDIENTS

- *4 large eggs*
- *1/4 cup milk*
- *1/2 cup diced bell peppers*
- *1/4 cup diced onions*

- *1/4 cup chopped spinach*
- *1/4 cup crumbled feta cheese*
- *Salt and pepper, to taste*
- *Olive oil spray*

INSTRUCTIONS

1. In a bowl, whisk together eggs, milk, salt, and pepper.
2. Stir in bell peppers, onions, spinach, and feta cheese.
3. Preheat the air fryer to 360°F (182°C).
4. Coat the basket of the air fryer with olive oil.
5. Pour the egg mixture into the basket.
6. Cook for about 8 minutes or until the omelette is set and lightly golden.
7. Carefully remove and serve warm.

Nutritional Value (per serving): Calories: 215, Fat: 14g, Carbohydrates: 6g, Protein: 16g

---

Air Fryer Herbed Mediterranean Potatoes

Preparation Time: 10 minutes   **Servings:** 4
Cooking Time: 20 minutes

INGREDIENTS

- *4 medium-sized potatoes, diced*

- *1 tbsp olive oil*

- *1 tsp dried rosemary*
- *1 tsp dried thyme*
- *1/2 tsp garlic powder*
- *Salt and pepper, to taste*

INSTRUCTIONS

1. In a large bowl, toss diced potatoes with olive oil, rosemary, thyme, garlic powder, salt, and pepper.
2. Preheat the air fryer to 380°F (193°C).
3. Place the seasoned potatoes in the air fryer basket.
4. Cook for 20 minutes, shaking the basket halfway through.
5. Serve hot as a hearty breakfast side.

Nutritional Value (per serving): Calories: 150, Fat: 3.5g, Carbohydrates: 27g, Protein: 3g

---

Air Fryer Mediterranean Breakfast Wraps

Preparation Time: 10 minutes

Cooking Time: 5 minutes

Servings: 2

INGREDIENTS

- *2 whole wheat tortillas*
- *4 eggs, scrambled*
- *1/2 cup cooked spinach*
- *1/4 cup chopped tomatoes*
- *1/4 cup crumbled feta cheese*
- *Salt and pepper, to taste*
- *Olive oil spray*

INSTRUCTIONS

1. Prepare scrambled eggs and set aside.
2. Lay out tortillas and evenly distribute scrambled eggs, spinach, tomatoes, and feta cheese on each.
3. Season with salt and pepper.
4. Roll up the tortillas tightly.
5. Preheat the air fryer to 360°F (182°C).
6. Coat the basket of the air fryer with olive oil and place the wraps seam side down.
7. Cook for 5 minutes or until golden and crispy.
8. Serve warm.

Nutritional Value (per serving): Calories: 320, Fat: 15g, Carbohydrates: 28g, Protein: 18g

---

Air Fryer Mediterranean Avocado and Egg Toast

Preparation Time: 5 minutes
Cooking Time: 8 minutes

Servings: 2

INGREDIENTS

- 2 slices whole grain bread
- 1 avocado, mashed
- 2 eggs
-

- Salt and pepper, to taste
- Olive oil spray

INSTRUCTIONS

1. Place bread slices in the air fryer basket and cook at 360°F (182°C) for 3 minutes until lightly toasted.
2. Remove bread and spread mashed avocado on each slice.
3. Crack an egg on top of each avocado toast.
4. Season with salt and pepper.
5. Return to the air fryer and cook at 370°F (188°C) for about 5 minutes or until eggs are cooked to your liking.
6. Serve immediately.

Nutritional Value (per serving): Calories: 300, Fat: 20g, Carbohydrates: 23g, Protein: 12g

---

Air Fryer Mediterranean Veggie and Feta Scramble

Preparation Time: 5 minutes
Cooking Time: 10 minutes

Servings: 2

INGREDIENTS

- 4 eggs, beaten
- 1/4 cup milk
- 1/2 cup diced zucchini
- 1/2 cup diced red bell pepper

- 1/4 cup crumbled feta cheese
- Salt and pepper, to taste
- Olive oil spray

INSTRUCTIONS

1. In a bowl, whisk together eggs, milk, salt, and pepper.
2. Stir in zucchini, bell pepper, and feta cheese.
3. Preheat the air fryer to 360°F (182°C).
4. Coat the basket of the air fryer with olive oil.

5. Place the egg mixture into the basket.
6. Cook for about 10 minutes, stirring halfway through, until the eggs are set.
7. Serve warm.

Nutritional Value (per serving): Calories: 215, Fat: 15g, Carbohydrates: 6g, Protein: 16g

---

Air Fryer Mediterranean Stuffed Avocados

Preparation Time: 10 minutes
Cooking Time: 5 minutes

Servings: 2

INGREDIENTS

- *2 ripe avocados, halved and pitted*
- *4 eggs*
- *Salt and pepper, to taste*
- *1/4 cup crumbled feta cheese*

- *1/4 cup diced cherry tomatoes*
- *2 tbsp chopped parsley*
- *Olive oil spray*

INSTRUCTIONS

1. Scoop out some of the avocado flesh to create a larger cavity.
2. Gently break one egg into each avocado half.
3. Season with salt and pepper.
4. Preheat the air fryer to 370°F (188°C).
5. Coat the basket of the air fryer with olive oil and place the avocado halves in the basket.
6. Cook for about 5 minutes or until the egg whites are whipped but yolks are still runny.
7. Garnish with feta cheese, cherry tomatoes, and parsley.
8. Serve immediately.

Nutritional Value (per serving): Calories: 345, Fat: 27g, Carbohydrates: 17g, Protein: 14g

---

Air Fryer Mediterranean Sweet Potato Hash

Preparation Time: 10 minutes
Cooking Time: 15 minutes

Servings: 4

INGREDIENTS

- *2 large sweet potatoes, peeled and diced*
- *1 red bell pepper, diced*

- *1 small red onion, diced*
- *2 cloves garlic, minced*

- *1 tsp smoked paprika*
- *1/2 tsp cumin*
- *Salt and pepper, to taste*
- *2 tbsp olive oil*
- *1/4 cup chopped fresh cilantro*

INSTRUCTIONS

1. In a bowl, toss sweet potatoes, bell pepper, onion, garlic, smoked paprika, cumin, salt, pepper, and olive oil.
2. Preheat the air fryer to 400°F (204°C).
3. Spread the sweet potato mixture in the air fryer basket.
4. Cook for 15 minutes, stirring halfway through, until potatoes are tender.
5. Garnish with fresh cilantro before serving.

Nutritional Value (per serving): Calories: 190, Fat: 7g, Carbohydrates: 30g, Protein: 3g

---

Air Fryer Lemon-Garlic Asparagus

Preparation Time: 5 minutes
Cooking Time: 8 minutes

Servings: 4

INGREDIENTS

- *1 lb fresh asparagus, ends trimmed*
- *2 tbsp olive oil*
- *2 cloves garlic, minced*
- *Zest of 1 lemon*
- *Salt and pepper, to taste*
- *Lemon wedges, for serving*

INSTRUCTIONS

1. In a bowl, toss asparagus with olive oil, garlic, lemon zest, salt, and pepper.
2. Preheat the air fryer to 380°F (193°C).
3. Place the asparagus in the air fryer basket.
4. Cook for 8 minutes or until asparagus is lightly browned and tender.
5. Serve with lemon wedges.

Nutritional Value (per serving): Calories: 80, Fat: 7g, Carbohydrates: 5g, Protein: 3g

---

Air Fryer Mediterranean Breakfast Bruschetta

Preparation Time: 10 minutes
Cooking Time: 5 minutes

Servings: 4

INGREDIENTS

- 4 slices whole grain bread
- 2 ripe tomatoes, diced
- 1/4 cup red onion, finely chopped
- 1 clove garlic, minced
- 2 tbsp chopped basil
- 1 tbsp balsamic vinegar
- Salt and pepper, to taste
- Olive oil spray

INSTRUCTIONS

1. In a bowl, mix tomatoes, red onion, garlic, basil, balsamic vinegar, salt, and pepper.
2. Preheat the air fryer to 360°F (182°C).
3. Spray both sides of the bread with olive oil.
4. Place bread slices in the air fryer basket and cook for 3 minutes, flipping halfway, until crispy.
5. Top each bread slice with the tomato mixture, and serve immediately.

Nutritional Value (per serving): Calories: 120, Fat: 2g, Carbohydrates: 22g, Protein: 4g

---

Air Fryer Zucchini and Feta Fritters

Preparation Time: 15 minutes
Cooking Time: 10 minutes

Servings: 4

INGREDIENTS

- 2 medium zucchinis, grated
- 1/2 cup crumbled feta cheese
- 1 egg, beaten
- 1/4 cup whole wheat flour
- 1/4 cup chopped dill
- Salt and pepper, to taste
- Olive oil spray

INSTRUCTIONS

1. Squeeze excess moisture out of grated zucchini using a clean towel.
2. In a bowl, combine zucchini, feta, egg, flour, dill, salt, and pepper.
3. Form into small patties.
4. Preheat the air fryer to 380°F (193°C).
5. Spray both the air fryer basket and the fritters with olive oil.
6. Cook for 10 minutes, flipping halfway, until golden and crispy.

Nutritional Value (per serving): Calories: 120, Fat: 6g, Carbohydrates: 10g, Protein: 7g

Chapter 4
Light Bites and Snacks

Air-Fried Stuffed Olives

Preparation Time: 15 minutes
Cooking Time: 10 minutes

Servings: 4

INGREDIENTS

- *Green olives (pitted): 1 cup (150g)*
- *Cream cheese: 1/2 cup (115g)*
- *Lemon zest: 1 tsp*

- *Bread crumbs: 1 cup (120g)*
- *Eggs (beaten): 2*

INSTRUCTIONS

1. Stuff each olive with a small amount of cream cheese mixed with lemon zest.
2. Dip in beaten egg, then in breadcrumbs.
3. Air fry at 375°F (190°C) for 10 minutes or until golden.
4. Serve with tzatziki sauce.

Nutritional Value (per serving): Calories: 180, Total Fat: 10g, Carbohydrates: 15g, Protein: 5g

---

Mediterranean Veggie Chips

Preparation Time: 10 minutes
Cooking Time: 12 minutes

Servings: 4

INGREDIENTS

- *Zucchini (thinly sliced): 1 cup (150g)*
- *Eggplant (thinly sliced): 1 cup (150g)*
- *Olive oil: 2 tbsp (30ml)*

- *Sea salt: to taste*
- *Paprika: to taste*

INSTRUCTIONS

1. Brush zucchini and eggplant slices with olive oil.
2. Season with salt and paprika.
3. Air fry at 350°F (175°C) for 10-12 minutes or until crispy.
4. Serve immediately.

Nutritional Value (per serving): Calories: 90, Total Fat: 7g, Carbohydrates: 8g, Protein: 2g

Feta-Stuffed Mini Bell Peppers

Preparation Time: 15 minutes
Cooking Time: 8 minutes

Servings: 4

INGREDIENTS

- *Mini bell peppers: 8*
- *Feta cheese (crumbled): 1/2 cup (115g)*
- *Olive tapenade: 2 tbsp (30ml)*
- *Olive oil: for brushing*

INSTRUCTIONS

1. Cut off the tops of the peppers and remove the seeds.
2. Mix feta and tapenade.
3. Stuff peppers with the feta mixture.
4. Brush with olive oil.
5. Air fry at 370°F (188°C) for 8 minutes.
6. Serve warm.

Nutritional Value (per serving): Calories: 150, Total Fat: 11g, Carbohydrates: 10g, Protein: 4g

---

Mediterranean Air-Fried Falafel

Preparation Time: 20 minutes (plus soaking time)

Cooking Time: 15 minutes
Servings: 4

INGREDIENTS

- *Chickpeas (soaked overnight): 2 cups (340g)*
- *Fresh parsley (chopped): 1/2 cup (30g)*
- *Garlic cloves: 2*
- *Ground cumin: 1 tsp*
- *Ground coriander: 1 tsp*
- *Salt: to taste*
- *Olive oil: for brushing*

INSTRUCTIONS

1. Blend chickpeas, parsley, garlic, cumin, coriander, and salt until a coarse paste forms.
2. Shape into balls.
3. Brush falafel balls with olive oil.
4. Air fry at 375°F (190°C) for 15 minutes.
5. Serve with yogurt sauce or tahini.

Nutritional Value (per serving): Calories: 210, Total Fat: 7g, Carbohydrates: 29g, Protein: 9g

Air-Fried Bruschetta Bites

Preparation Time: 10 minutes   **Servings: 4**
Cooking Time: 5 minutes

INGREDIENTS

- *Whole grain baguette (sliced): 8 pieces*
- *Cherry tomatoes (chopped): 1 cup (150g)*
- *Olive oil: 2 tbsp (30ml) plus extra for brushing*
- *Fresh basil (chopped): 2 tbsp (10g)*
- *Garlic clove (minced): 1*
- *Salt and pepper: to taste*

INSTRUCTIONS

1. Brush baguette slices with olive oil.
2. Air fry at 370°F (188°C) for 3-5 minutes until crisp.
3. Mix tomatoes, 2 tbsp olive oil, basil, garlic, salt, and pepper.
4. Cover each slice of baguettes with the tomato mixture.
5. Serve immediately.

Nutritional Value (per serving): Calories: 200, Total Fat: 10g, Carbohydrates: 24g, Protein: 4g

---

Air-Fried Greek Meatballs (Keftedes)

Preparation Time: 20 minutes   **Servings: 4**
Cooking Time: 15 minutes

INGREDIENTS

- *Ground lamb: 1 lb (450g)*
- *Fresh mint (chopped): 2 tbsp (10g)*
- *Red onion (finely chopped): 1/2*
- *Garlic cloves (minced): 2*
- *Feta cheese (crumbled): 1/4 cup (60g)*
- *Olive oil: for brushing*
- *Salt and pepper: to taste*

INSTRUCTIONS

1. Combine lamb, mint, onion, garlic, feta, salt, and pepper in a bowl.
2. Shape mixture into small meatballs.
3. Brush meatballs with olive oil.
4. Air fry at 375°F (190°C) for 15 minutes, or until cooked through.
5. Serve with tzatziki sauce.

Nutritional Value (per serving): Calories: 320, Total Fat: 23g, Carbohydrates: 2g, Protein: 24g

Air-Fried Spinach and Cheese Triangles

Preparation Time: 25 minutes
Cooking Time: 12 minutes

Servings: 4

INGREDIENTS

- *Phyllo dough: 8 sheets*
- *Fresh spinach (chopped): 2 cups (60g)*
- *Feta cheese (crumbled): 1 cup (230g)*

- *Egg (beaten): 1*
- *Nutmeg: a pinch*
- *Olive oil: for brushing*

INSTRUCTIONS

1. Mix spinach, feta, egg, and nutmeg in a bowl.
2. Lay a phyllo sheet, brush with olive oil, and place another sheet on top. Cut vertically into 3 strips.
3. Fill each strip with a dollop of filling and fold into a triangle.
4. Brush triangles with more olive oil.
5. Air fry at 375°F (190°C) for 12 minutes, or until golden.
6. Serve warm.

Nutritional Value (per serving): Calories: 260, Total Fat: 12g, Carbohydrates: 28g, Protein: 10g

---

Mediterranean Hummus Cups

Preparation Time: 15 minutes
Cooking Time: 8 minutes

Servings: 4

INGREDIENTS

- *Mini tortilla cups: 12*
- *Hummus: 1 cup (240g)*
- *Cucumber (diced): 1/2 cup (80g)*

- *Cherry tomatoes (quartered): 1/2 cup (75g)*
- *Kalamata olives (chopped): 1/4 cup (40g)*
- *Feta cheese (crumbled): 1/4 cup (60g)*

INSTRUCTIONS

1. Air fry tortilla cups at 350°F (175°C) for 5 minutes.
2. Fill each cup with hummus, then top with tomatoes, cucumber, olives, and feta.
3. Serve immediately.

Nutritional Value (per serving): Calories: 210, Total Fat: 9g, Carbohydrates: 25g, Protein: 8g

Air-Fried Mediterranean Quesadillas

Preparation Time: 10 minutes
Cooking Time: 8 minutes

Servings: 4

INGREDIENTS

- Tortillas: 8
- Mozzarella cheese (shredded): 1 cup (115g)
- Sun-dried tomatoes (chopped): 1/2 cup (75g)
- Black olives (sliced): 1/3 cup (50g)
- Fresh basil (chopped): 1/4 cup (15g)

INSTRUCTIONS

1. Lay a tortilla, sprinkle with cheese, tomatoes, olives, and basil. Cover with another tortilla.
2. Air fry at 375°F (190°C) for 8 minutes, flipping halfway.
3. Cut into wedges and serve with tzatziki sauce.

Nutritional Value (per serving): Calories: 310, Total Fat: 12g, Carbohydrates: 38g, Protein: 12g

---

Air-Fried Mediterranean Stuffed Mushrooms

Preparation Time: 15 minutes
Cooking Time: 10 minutes

Servings: 4

INGREDIENTS

- Large mushrooms: 16
- Ricotta cheese: 1/2 cup (120g)
- Spinach (chopped): 1 cup (30g)
- Garlic cloves (minced): 2
- Olive oil: 2 tbsp (30ml)
- Parmesan cheese (grated): 1/4 cup (25g)
- Salt and pepper: to taste

INSTRUCTIONS

1. Remove stems from mushrooms and brush caps with olive oil.
2. In a bowl, mix ricotta, spinach, garlic, parmesan, salt, and pepper.
3. Fill each mushroom cap halfway with the ricotta mixture.
4. Air fry at 375°F (190°C) for 10 minutes.
5. Serve warm.

Nutritional Value (per serving): Calories: 180, Total Fat: 11g, Carbohydrates: 10g, Protein: 8g

Air-Fried Olive Tapenade Crostini

Preparation Time: 10 minutes
Cooking Time: 5 minutes

Servings: 4

INGREDIENTS

- *Baguette (sliced): 16 pieces*
- *Green olives (pitted): 1 cup (150g)*
- *Black olives (pitted): 1 cup (150g)*
- *Capers: 2 tbsp (30g)*
- *Olive oil: 1/4 cup (60ml)*
- *Garlic cloves: 2*
- *Fresh parsley (chopped): 2 tbsp (8g)*

INSTRUCTIONS

1. In a food processor, combine olives, capers, olive oil, garlic, and parsley. Blend until smooth.
2. Brush baguette slices with olive oil.
3. Air fry at 375°F (190°C) for 5 minutes or until crispy.
4. Spread olive tapenade on each crostini.
5. Serve immediately.

Nutritional Value (per serving): Calories: 220, Total Fat: 10g, Carbohydrates: 28g, Protein: 4g

---

Mediterranean Zucchini Fritters (1st Version)

Preparation Time: 20 minutes
Cooking Time: 10 minutes

Servings: 4

INGREDIENTS

- *Zucchini (grated): 2 large*
- *Feta cheese (crumbled): 1/2 cup (115g)*
- *Fresh dill (chopped): 2 tbsp (10g)*
- *Egg: 1*
- *All-purpose flour: 1/2 cup (60g)*
- *Salt and pepper: to taste*
- *Olive oil: for brushing*

INSTRUCTIONS

1. Place grated zucchini in a colander and sprinkle with salt. Let it sit for 10 minutes, then squeeze out excess moisture.
2. In a bowl, combine zucchini, feta, dill, egg, flour, salt, and pepper.
3. Shape mixture into small patties.
4. Brush each patty with olive oil.

5. Air fry at 375°F (190°C) for 10 minutes, flipping halfway through.
6. Serve with a dollop of tzatziki sauce.

Nutritional Value (per serving): Calories: 210, Total Fat: 10g, Carbohydrates: 20g, Protein: 8g

---

Air-Fried Mediterranean Stuffed Peppers (1st Version)

Preparation Time: 20 minutes   **Servings:** 4
Cooking Time: 12 minutes

INGREDIENTS

- *Mini bell peppers: 12*
- *Cooked quinoa: 1 cup (185g)*
- *Cherry tomatoes (chopped): 1/2 cup (75g)*
- *Kalamata olives (chopped): 1/4 cup (40g)*
- *Feta cheese (crumbled): 1/2 cup (115g)*
- *Olive oil: 1 tbsp (15ml)*

INSTRUCTIONS

1. Slice off the tops of the peppers and remove seeds.
2. In a bowl, mix quinoa, tomatoes, olives, feta, and olive oil.
3. Stuff each pepper with the quinoa mixture.
4. Air fry at 375°F (190°C) for 12 minutes or until peppers are tender.
5. Serve warm.

Nutritional Value (per serving): Calories: 230, Total Fat: 11g, Carbohydrates: 27g, Protein: 7g

Chapter 5

Vegetables and Sides

The Mediterranean's focus on vegetables has deep historical and cultural roots. Historically, meat was a luxury in this region, kept for special events and feasts. In its stead, vegetables, grains, and legumes formed the everyday staples. And while times have changed, the central role of vegetables remains unfazed, celebrated not as a necessity borne from scarcity, but as a choice that aligns with health and sustainability.

The science is unequivocal. A vegetable-rich diet has numerous health benefits. They are brimming with essential nutrients, antioxidants, and dietary fiber – elements known to reduce the risk of chronic diseases, aid digestion, and foster overall health. The Mediterranean people, with their lower incidences of heart disease and longer life expectancies, are a living testament to these benefits.

Crispy Mediterranean Brussels Sprouts

Preparation Time: 10 minutes
Cooking Time: 15 minutes

Servings: 4

INGREDIENTS

- *Brussels sprouts (halved): 500g*
- *Olive oil: 2 tbsp (30ml)*
- *Fresh lemon zest: 1 tbsp*

- *Feta cheese (crumbled): 50g*
- *Garlic powder: 1 tsp*
- *Salt and pepper: to taste*

INSTRUCTIONS

1. In a bowl, toss Brussels sprouts with olive oil, garlic powder, salt, and pepper.
2. Place in the air fryer basket.
3. Cook at 375°F (190°C) for 15 minutes or until golden brown and crispy.
4. Transfer to a bowl and toss with lemon zest.
5. Garnish with crumbled feta cheese before serving.

Nutritional Value (per serving): Calories: 125, Total Fat: 7g, Carbohydrates: 12g, Protein: 5g

---

Mediterranean Potato Wedges

Preparation Time: 10 minutes
Cooking Time: 20 minutes

Servings: 4

INGREDIENTS

- *Large russet potatoes (cut into wedges): 2*
- *Olive oil: 3 tbsp (45ml)*
- *Dried rosemary: 1 tsp*

- *Dried thyme: 1 tsp*
- *Sea salt: to taste*
- *Grated parmesan: 50g*

INSTRUCTIONS

1. In a bowl, toss potato wedges with olive oil, rosemary, thyme, and sea salt.
2. Spread the wedges in the air fryer basket.
3. Cook at 400°F (200°C) for 20 minutes, turning halfway through.
4. Sprinkle with grated parmesan before serving.

Nutritional Value (per serving): Calories: 215, Total Fat: 10g, Carbohydrates: 27g, Protein: 5g

Air-Fried Mediterranean Asparagus

Preparation Time: 5 minutes   **Servings:** 4
Cooking Time: 10 minutes

INGREDIENTS

- Fresh asparagus spears: 500g
- Olive oil: 2 tbsp (30ml)
- Lemon juice: 1 tbsp
- Salt and pepper: to taste
- Toasted almond slices: 50g

INSTRUCTIONS

1. Trim the tough ends of the asparagus and toss them in olive oil, lemon juice, salt, and pepper.
2. Place the spears in the air fryer basket.
3. Cook at 375°F (190°C) for 10 minutes.
4. Serve with toasted almond on top.

Nutritional Value (per serving): Calories: 115, Total Fat: 9g, Carbohydrates: 7g, Protein: 4g

---

Air Fryer Eggplant Rounds

Preparation Time: 10 minutes   **Servings:** 4
Cooking Time: 15 minutes

INGREDIENTS

- *Eggplant (sliced into rounds): 1 large*
- *Olive oil: 2 tbsp (30ml)*
- *Dried oregano: 1 tsp*
- *Sea salt: to taste*
- *Grated parmesan: 50g*

INSTRUCTIONS

1. Brush each eggplant round with olive oil and sprinkle with oregano and sea salt.
2. Lay the rounds in the air fryer basket without overlapping.
3. Cook at 375°F (190°C) for 15 minutes or until golden and crispy.
4. Garnish with grated parmesan before serving.

Nutritional Value (per serving): Calories: 115, Total Fat: 8g, Carbohydrates: 10g, Protein: 4g

Mediterranean Roasted Red Peppers

Preparation Time: 5 minutes   **Servings:** 4
Cooking Time: 12 minutes

INGREDIENTS

- *Large red bell peppers (quartered): 2*
- *Olive oil: 2 tbsp (30ml)*
- *Minced garlic: 1 tsp*
- *Sea salt: to taste*
- *Crumbled feta cheese: 50g*

INSTRUCTIONS

1. Toss red pepper quarters with olive oil, minced garlic, and sea salt.
2. Lay them skin-side down in the air fryer basket.
3. Cook at 375°F (190°C) for 12 minutes or until softened.
4. Garnish with crumbled feta before serving.

Nutritional Value (per serving): Calories: 95, Total Fat: 7g, Carbohydrates: 7g, Protein: 3g

---

Crispy Mediterranean Zucchini Fritters (2nd Version)

Preparation Time: 15 minutes   **Servings:** 4
Cooking Time: 12 minutes

INGREDIENTS

- *Zucchini (grated and drained): 2 medium*
- *Feta cheese (crumbled): 100g*
- *Egg: 1*
- *All-purpose flour: 2 tbsp (30ml)*
- *Fresh mint (chopped): 1 tbsp*
- *Olive oil: 1 tbsp (15ml)*
- *Salt and pepper: to taste*

INSTRUCTIONS

1. In a bowl, combine grated zucchini, crumbled feta, egg, flour, and mint. Season with salt and pepper.
2. Form the mixture into small patties.
3. Brush each patty with olive oil and place them in the air fryer basket.
4. Cook at 375°F (190°C) for 12 minutes, flipping halfway through.
5. Serve warm with your favorite dipping sauce.

Nutritional Value (per serving): Calories: 135, Total Fat: 7g, Carbohydrates: 10g, Protein: 6g

Garlic & Lemon Broccoli Florets

Preparation Time: 10 minutes
Cooking Time: 10 minutes

Servings: 4

INGREDIENTS

- Fresh broccoli florets: 500g
- Olive oil: 2 tbsp (30ml)
- Garlic (minced): 2 cloves
- Fresh lemon zest: 1 tsp
- Salt and pepper: to taste

INSTRUCTIONS

1. Toss broccoli florets with olive oil, minced garlic, lemon zest, salt, and pepper.
2. Place in the air fryer basket.
3. Cook at 375°F (190°C) for 10 minutes or until edges are crispy.
4. Serve immediately.

Nutritional Value (per serving): Calories: 90, Total Fat: 5g, Carbohydrates: 8g, Protein: 3g

---

Air Fryer Mediterranean Cauliflower Steaks

Preparation Time: 10 minutes
Cooking Time: 14 minutes

Servings: 4

INGREDIENTS

- *Cauliflower (sliced into 1-inch thick steaks): 1 medium*
- *Olive oil: 2 tbsp (30ml)*

- *Dried rosemary: 1 tsp*
- *Sea salt and pepper: to taste*
- *Fresh parsley (chopped): for garnish*

INSTRUCTIONS

1. Brush cauliflower steaks with olive oil and sprinkle with rosemary, sea salt, and pepper.
2. Lay the steaks in the air fryer basket without overlapping.
3. Cook at 400°F (200°C) for 14 minutes, turning halfway through.
4. Garnish with chopped parsley before serving.

Nutritional Value (per serving): Calories: 65, Total Fat: 5g, Carbohydrates: 6g, Protein: 2g

---

Stuffed Mediterranean Bell Peppers

Preparation Time: 15 minutes
Cooking Time: 18 minutes

Servings: 4

INGREDIENTS

- *Bell peppers (tops removed and deseeded): 4*
- *Cooked quinoa: 1 cup (250ml)*
- *Kalamata olives (chopped): 50g*
- *Cherry tomatoes (halved): 100g*

- *Feta cheese (crumbled): 100g*
- *Olive oil: 1 tbsp (15ml)*
- *Fresh basil (chopped): 1 tbsp*
- *Salt and pepper: to taste*

INSTRUCTIONS

1. In a bowl, mix quinoa, olives, cherry tomatoes, feta cheese, and basil. Season with salt and pepper.
2. Fill each bell pepper halfway with the quinoa mixture.
3. Place stuffed peppers upright in the air fryer basket.
4. Drizzle with olive oil.
5. Cook at 375°F (190°C) for 18 minutes or until peppers are tender.
6. Serve hot.

Nutritional Value (per serving): Calories: 225, Total Fat: 9g, Carbohydrates: 28g, Protein: 8g

---

Mediterranean Beet Fries

Preparation Time: 10 minutes
Cooking Time: 15 minutes

Servings: 4

INGREDIENTS

- *Fresh beets (peeled and sliced into fries): 4 medium*
- *Olive oil: 2 tbsp (30ml)*

- *Sea salt: to taste*
- *Fresh dill (chopped): 1 tbsp*

INSTRUCTIONS

1. Toss beet fries with olive oil and sea salt.
2. Spread the fries in the air fryer basket.
3. Cook at 375°F (190°C) for 15 minutes, shaking the basket occasionally.
4. Garnish with fresh dill before serving.

Nutritional Value (per serving): Calories: 85, Total Fat: 7g, Carbohydrates: 6g, Protein: 1g

Chapter 6

Poultry and Meat

Lemon-Oregano Chicken Thighs

Preparation Time: 10 minutes   **Servings: 4**
Cooking Time: 22 minutes

INGREDIENTS

- Chicken thighs (boneless, skinless): 4 pieces
- Olive oil: 2 tbsp (30ml)
- Fresh lemon juice: 2 tbsp (30ml)
- Dried oregano: 2 tsp
- Garlic (minced): 3 cloves
- Salt and pepper: to taste
- Fresh parsley (chopped): for garnish

INSTRUCTIONS

1. In a bowl, whisk together olive oil, lemon juice, oregano, garlic, salt, and pepper.
2. Coat chicken thighs with the marinade and let sit for at least 15 minutes.
3. Place marinated thighs in the air fryer basket.
4. Cook at 380°F (195°C) for 22 minutes, flipping halfway.
5. Garnish with fresh parsley before serving.

Nutritional Value (per serving): Calories: 240, Total Fat: 15g, Carbohydrates: 2g, Protein: 24g

---

Air Fryer Mediterranean Turkey Patties

Preparation Time: 15 minutes   **Servings: 4**
Cooking Time: 15 minutes

INGREDIENTS

- *Ground turkey: 1 lb (450g)*
- *Feta cheese (crumbled): 1/2 cup (125ml)*
- *Sun-dried tomatoes (chopped): 1/4 cup (60ml)*
- *Fresh basil (chopped): 2 tbsp*
- *Olive oil: 1 tbsp (15ml)*
- *Salt and pepper: to taste*

INSTRUCTIONS

1. In a bowl, combine ground turkey, feta, sun-dried tomatoes, basil, salt, and pepper. Mix well.
2. Form mixture into four patties.

3. Brush patties with olive oil.
4. Cook in the air fryer at 375°F (190°C) for 15 minutes, flipping once.
5. Serve with a yogurt-based sauce or fresh salad.

Nutritional Value (per serving): Calories: 265, Total Fat: 12g, Carbohydrates: 4g, Protein: 32g

---

Mediterranean Herb-Infused Chicken Wings

Preparation Time: 10 minutes + marinating

Cooking Time: 24 minutes
Servings: 4

INGREDIENTS

- *Chicken wings: 2 lbs (900g)*
- *Olive oil: 2 tbsp (30ml)*
- *Fresh rosemary (minced): 2 tsp*

- *Fresh thyme (minced): 2 tsp*
- *Garlic (minced): 4 cloves*
- *Salt and pepper: to taste*

INSTRUCTIONS

1. In a large bowl, mix together olive oil, rosemary, thyme, garlic, salt, and pepper.
2. Toss chicken wings in the herb mixture and marinate for at least 30 minutes.
3. Arrange wings in the air fryer basket in a single layer.
4. Cook at 390°F (200°C) for 24 minutes, flipping halfway.
5. Serve with tzatziki or aioli dip.

Nutritional Value (per serving): Calories: 315, Total Fat: 23g, Carbohydrates: 1g, Protein: 26g

---

Air-Fried Greek Lemon Chicken Drumsticks

Preparation Time: 10 minutes + marinating

Cooking Time: 25 minutes
Servings: 4

INGREDIENTS

- *Chicken drumsticks: 8 pieces*
- *Olive oil: 2 tbsp (30ml)*
- *Fresh lemon juice: 3 tbsp (45ml)*

- *Dried oregano: 2 tsp*
- *Garlic (minced): 4 cloves*
- *Salt and pepper: to taste*

INSTRUCTIONS

1. Whisk together olive oil, lemon juice, oregano, garlic, salt, and pepper.
2. Marinate drumsticks in the mixture for at least an hour.
3. Place drumsticks in the air fryer basket.
4. Cook at 380°F (195°C) for 25 minutes, turning occasionally.
5. Serve with a side of Greek salad.

Nutritional Value (per serving): Calories: 265, Total Fat: 15g, Carbohydrates: 2g, Protein: 28g

---

Mediterranean Stuffed Chicken Breasts

Preparation Time: 20 minutes
Cooking Time: 25 minutes

Servings: 4

INGREDIENTS

- Chicken breasts (boneless, skinless): 4 pieces
- Spinach (chopped): 1 cup (250ml)
- Feta cheese: 1/2 cup (125ml)
- Sun-dried tomatoes (chopped): 1/4 cup (60ml)
- Olive oil: 2 tbsp (30ml)
- Salt and pepper: to taste

INSTRUCTIONS

1. Cut a pocket into each chicken breast.
2. In a bowl, mix spinach, feta, and sun-dried tomatoes.
3. Stuff each chicken breast with the mixture.
4. Coat the chicken with olive oil and season with salt and pepper.
5. Place in the air fryer basket.
6. Cook at 370°F (185°C) for 25 minutes.
7. Serve with roasted vegetables or salad.

Nutritional Value (per serving): Calories: 310, Total Fat: 13g, Carbohydrates: 5g, Protein: 39g

Air-Fryer Chicken Shawarma Wraps

Preparation Time: 15 minutes + marinating

Cooking Time: 20 minutes
Servings: 4

INGREDIENTS

- *Chicken thighs (boneless, skinless): 1 lb (450g)*
- *Olive oil: 2 tbsp (30ml)*
- *Ground cumin: 1 tsp*
- *Ground coriander: 1 tsp*
- *Ground paprika: 1 tsp*
- *Ground turmeric: 1/2 tsp*
- *Garlic (minced): 3 cloves*
- *Salt and pepper: to taste*
- *Pita bread: 4 pieces*
- *Tzatziki sauce and lettuce: for serving*

INSTRUCTIONS

1. Combine olive oil, spices, garlic, salt, and pepper in a bowl.
2. Marinate chicken in the spice mixture for at least 1 hour.
3. Place chicken in the air fryer basket.
4. Cook at 380°F (195°C) for 20 minutes or until cooked through.
5. Slice chicken and serve in pita bread with lettuce and tzatziki.

Nutritional Value (per serving): Calories: 375, Total Fat: 12g, Carbohydrates: 34g, Protein: 30g

---

Mediterranean Chicken Tenders with Tahini Dip

Preparation Time: 10 minutes + marinating

Cooking Time: 15 minutes
Servings: 4

INGREDIENTS

- *Chicken tenders: 1 lb (450g)*
- *Olive oil: 2 tbsp (30ml)*
- *Lemon juice: 1 tbsp (15ml)*
- *Ground sumac: 1 tsp*
- *Garlic (minced): 2 cloves*
- *Salt and pepper: to taste*
- *Tahini: 1/2 cup (125ml)*
- *Water: 2 tbsp (30ml)*

INSTRUCTIONS

1. Mix olive oil, lemon juice, sumac, garlic, salt, and pepper in a bowl.
2. Marinate chicken tenders for at least 30 minutes.
3. Place chicken in the air fryer basket.
4. Cook at 375°F (190°C) for 15 minutes, turning once.

5. Combine tahini and water to create a dip.
6. Serve chicken tenders with tahini dip on the side.

Nutritional Value (per serving): Calories: 340, Total Fat: 18g, Carbohydrates: 5g, Protein: 37g

---

Air-Fryer Mediterranean Herb Chicken Skewers

Preparation Time: 15 minutes + marinating

Cooking Time: 20 minutes
Servings: 4

INGREDIENTS

- *Chicken breasts (cubed): 1 lb (450g)*
- *Olive oil: 2 tbsp (30ml)*
- *Fresh basil (chopped): 2 tbsp*
- *Fresh rosemary (chopped): 2 tbsp*
- *Fresh thyme (chopped): 2 tbsp*
- *Lemon zest: from 1 lemon*
- *Salt and pepper: to taste*

INSTRUCTIONS

1. Combine olive oil, herbs, lemon zest, salt, and pepper in a bowl.
2. Marinate chicken cubes for 1-2 hours.
3. Skewer chicken cubes and place in the air fryer basket.
4. Cook at 380°F (195°C) for 20 minutes, turning once.
5. Serve skewers with a side of roasted vegetables or salad.

Nutritional Value (per serving): Calories: 220, Total Fat: 8g, Carbohydrates: 1g, Protein: 32g

---

Air-Fryer Chicken Meatballs with Feta and Spinach

Preparation Time: 20 minutes
Cooking Time: 15 minutes

Servings: 4

INGREDIENTS

- *Ground chicken: 1 lb (450g)*
- *Spinach (finely chopped): 1/2 cup (125ml)*
- *Feta cheese (crumbled): 1/2 cup (125ml)*
- *Bread crumbs: 1/4 cup (60ml)*
- *Egg: 1*
- *Olive oil: 1 tbsp (15ml)*
- *Salt and pepper: to taste*

1. Combine chicken, spinach, feta, bread crumbs, egg, salt, and pepper in a bowl.
2. Shape into meatballs and brush with olive oil.
3. Place meatballs in the air fryer basket.
4. Cook at 375°F (190°C) for 15 minutes or until golden brown.
5. Serve with a yogurt-based dip or tomato sauce.

Nutritional Value (per serving): Calories: 280, Total Fat: 14g, Carbohydrates: 10g, Protein: 28g

---

Air-Fryer Mediterranean Spiced Chicken Legs

Preparation Time: 10 minutes + marinating

Cooking Time: 25 minutes
Servings: 4

INGREDIENTS

- Chicken legs: 4
- Olive oil: 2 tbsp (30ml)
- Ground cumin: 1 tsp
- Ground coriander: 1 tsp
- Ground paprika: 1 tsp
- Garlic (minced): 3 cloves
- Salt and pepper: to taste

INSTRUCTIONS

1. Combine olive oil, spices, garlic, salt, and pepper in a bowl.
2. Marinate chicken legs with this mixture for at least 1 hour.
3. Place chicken legs in the air fryer basket.
4. Cook at 370°F (185°C) for 25 minutes, turning once.
5. Serve with a salad or a side of roasted vegetables.

Nutritional Value (per serving): Calories: 320, Total Fat: 19g, Carbohydrates: 2g, Protein: 34g

---

Air-Fryer Mediterranean Lamb Chops

Preparation Time: 15 minutes + marinating

Cooking Time: 15 minutes
Servings: 4

INGREDIENTS

- *Lamb chops: 8*
- *Olive oil: 3 tbsp (45ml)*
- *Fresh rosemary: 2 sprigs*
- *Garlic (minced): 4 cloves*
- *Lemon juice: 2 tbsp (30ml)*
- *Salt and pepper: to taste*

INSTRUCTIONS

1. Combine olive oil, rosemary, garlic, lemon juice, salt, and pepper in a bowl. Marinate lamb chops for at least 1 hour.
2. Place lamb chops in the air fryer basket.
3. Cook at 375°F (190°C) for 15 minutes, turning once.
4. Serve with roasted Mediterranean vegetables.

Nutritional Value (per serving): Calories: 385, Total Fat: 27g, Carbohydrates: 1g, Protein: 29g

---

Air-Fryer Herb-Crusted Pork Tenderloin

Preparation Time: 20 minutes + marinating

Cooking Time: 20 minutes
Servings: 4

INGREDIENTS

- *Pork tenderloin: 1 lb (450g)*
- *Olive oil: 2 tbsp (30ml)*
- *Fresh thyme (chopped): 2 tsp*
- *Fresh rosemary (chopped): 2 tsp*
- *Fresh oregano (chopped): 2 tsp*
- *Salt and pepper: to taste*

INSTRUCTIONS

1. Mix olive oil, herbs, salt, and pepper. Coat the pork tenderloin with the mixture and let marinate for 1-2 hours.
2. Place the pork tenderloin in the air fryer basket.
3. Cook at 365°F (185°C) for 20 minutes.
4. Let it rest for a few minutes before slicing and serve.

Nutritional Value (per serving): Calories: 215, Total Fat: 9g, Carbohydrates: 1g, Protein: 29g

---

Air-Fryer Mediterranean Beef Kebabs

Preparation Time: 25 minutes + marinating

Cooking Time: 15 minutes
Servings: 4

INGREDIENTS

- Beef cubes: 1 lb (450g)
- Olive oil: 2 tbsp (30ml)
- Lemon zest: from 1 lemon
- Ground cumin: 1 tsp
- Ground coriander: 1 tsp
- Paprika: 1 tsp
- Garlic (minced): 3 cloves
- Salt and pepper: to taste

INSTRUCTIONS

1. Mix olive oil, lemon zest, spices, garlic, salt, and pepper in a bowl. Marinate beef cubes in this mixture for 1-2 hours.
2. Skewer the beef cubes and place them in the air fryer basket.
3. Cook at 375°F (190°C) for 15 minutes, turning halfway.
4. Serve with a Mediterranean salad and tzatziki sauce.

Nutritional Value (per serving): Calories: 265, Total Fat: 14g, Carbohydrates: 2g, Protein: 30g

---

Air-Fryer Beef and Veggie Mediterranean Platter

Preparation Time: 20 minutes
Cooking Time: 20 minutes

Servings: 4

INGREDIENTS

- *Beef strips: 1 lb (450g)*
- *Red bell pepper (sliced): 1*
- *Zucchini (sliced): 1*
- *Eggplant (sliced): 1/2*
- *Olive oil: 3 tbsp (45ml)*
- *Ground cumin: 1 tsp*
- *Ground coriander: 1 tsp*
- *Salt and pepper: to taste*

INSTRUCTIONS

1. In a bowl, combine beef strips, cumin, coriander, 2 tbsp of olive oil, salt, and pepper. Mix well.

2. In another bowl, toss the sliced veggies in salt, pepper, and 1 tbsp of olive oil.
3. Place beef and veggies in the air fryer basket.
4. Cook at 375°F (190°C) for 20 minutes, shaking the basket occasionally.
5. Serve with pita bread and a drizzle of tahini sauce.

Nutritional Value (per serving): Calories: 320, Total Fat: 18g, Carbohydrates: 12g, Protein: 28g

Air-Fryer Mediterranean Steak Fajitas

Preparation Time: 20 minutes + marinating

Cooking Time: 15 minutes
Servings: 4

INGREDIENTS

- Flank steak: 1 lb (450g), thinly sliced
- Red bell pepper: 1, thinly sliced
- Yellow bell pepper: 1, thinly sliced
- Onion: 1 medium, thinly sliced
- Olive oil: 2 tbsp (30ml)
- Lemon juice: 2 tbsp (30ml)
- Ground cumin: 1 tsp
- Garlic (minced): 3 cloves
- Salt and pepper: to taste

INSTRUCTIONS

1. Mix olive oil, lemon juice, cumin, garlic, salt, and pepper. Marinate steak slices in half of this mixture for 1 hour. Toss the vegetables in the remaining mixture.
2. Place the steak and vegetables in the air fryer basket, ensuring they are evenly distributed.
3. Cook at 375°F (190°C) for 12-15 minutes, shaking the basket halfway.
4. Serve on pita or tortillas with tzatziki or hummus.

Nutritional Value (per serving): Calories: 300, Total Fat: 14g, Carbohydrates: 9g, Protein: 30g

Air-Fryer Rosemary-Infused Beef Sliders

Preparation Time: 20 minutes
Cooking Time: 10 minutes

Servings: 4

INGREDIENTS

- *Ground beef: 1 lb (450g)*
- *Fresh rosemary: 1 tbsp, finely chopped*
- *Feta cheese: 1/2 cup, crumbled*
- *Olive oil: 1 tbsp (15ml)*
- *Salt and pepper: to taste*
- *Slider buns: 8*

INSTRUCTIONS

1. Combine beef, rosemary, feta cheese, olive oil, salt, and pepper. Form into small patties.
2. Place patties in the air fryer basket.
3. Cook at 370°F (185°C) for 10 minutes or until desired doneness.
4. Serve on slider buns with lettuce, tomato, and a drizzle of tzatziki.

Nutritional Value (per serving): Calories: 390, Total Fat: 24g, Carbohydrates: 20g, Protein: 24g

---

Air-Fryer Mediterranean Stuffed Peppers (2nd Version)

Preparation Time: 25 minutes
Cooking Time: 20 minutes

Servings: 4

INGREDIENTS

- *Bell peppers (any color): 4 large*
- *Ground beef: 1/2 lb (225g)*
- *Quinoa: 1 cup, cooked*
- *Cherry tomatoes: 1/2 cup, halved*
- *Olive oil: 2 tbsp (30ml)*
- *Garlic (minced): 2 cloves*
- *Salt and pepper: to taste*
- *Feta cheese: 1/4 cup, crumbled*

INSTRUCTIONS

1. Slice the tops off the peppers and remove seeds.
2. In a bowl, combine beef, olive oil, cooked quinoa, garlic, cherry tomatoes, salt, and pepper.
3. Fill each pepper halfway with the mixture and top with crumbled feta.
4. Place the stuffed peppers in the air fryer basket.
5. Cook at 350°F (175°C) for 20 minutes or until peppers are tender.
6. Serve with a side salad.

Nutritional Value (per serving): Calories: 330, Total Fat: 15g, Carbohydrates: 30g, Protein: 20g

Air-Fryer Beef-Stuffed Eggplants

Preparation Time: 25 minutes
Cooking Time: 25 minutes

Servings: 4

INGREDIENTS

- Eggplants: 2 medium
- Ground beef: 1/2 lb (225g)
- Onion: 1 small, finely chopped
- Olive oil: 2 tbsp (30ml)

- Fresh parsley: 2 tbsp, chopped
- Salt and pepper: to taste
- Mozzarella cheese: 1/2 cup, shredded

INSTRUCTIONS

1. Slice the eggplants in half lengthwise. Remove the flesh, leaving an edge of about 1/2-inch.
2. Chop the flesh and set aside.
3. In a skillet, heat olive oil and sauté onion until translucent. Add ground beef, eggplant flesh, salt, and pepper. Cook until beef is browned.
4. Stir in parsley and remove from heat.
5. Fill the eggplant shells with the beef mixture and top with shredded mozzarella.
6. Place the stuffed eggplants in the air fryer basket.
7. Cook at 350°F (175°C) for 25 minutes or until eggplants are tender and cheese is melted.
8. Garnish with additional parsley if desired.

Nutritional Value (per serving): Calories: 320, Total Fat: 18g, Carbohydrates: 22g, Protein: 22g

---

Air-Fryer Mediterranean Beef Skewers

Preparation Time: 25 minutes + marinating

Cooking Time: 15 minutes
Servings: 4

INGREDIENTS

- Beef chunks: 1 lb (450g)
- Red bell pepper: 1, cut into chunks
- Red onion: 1, cut into chunks
- Zucchini: 1, cut into chunks
- Olive oil: 3 tbsp (45ml)

- Lemon juice: 3 tbsp (45ml)
- Garlic (minced): 3 cloves
- Ground cumin: 1 tsp
- Ground coriander: 1 tsp
- Salt and pepper: to taste

INSTRUCTIONS

1. In a bowl, mix olive oil, lemon juice, garlic, cumin, coriander, salt, and pepper. Marinate beef chunks in this mixture for at least 2 hours.
2. Thread beef, peppers, onions, and zucchini onto skewers.
3. Place skewers in the air fryer basket.
4. Cook at 375°F (190°C) for 15 minutes, turning halfway.
5. Serve with hummus or a side of tzatziki.

Nutritional Value (per serving): Calories: 370, Total Fat: 22g, Carbohydrates: 12g, Protein: 30g

Chapter 7

Fish and Seafood

Air-Fryer Lemon-Herb Salmon Fillets

Preparation Time: 10 minutes
Cooking Time: 15 minutes

Servings: 4

INGREDIENTS

- Salmon fillets: 4 (6 oz/170g each)
- Olive oil: 2 tbsp (30ml)
- Lemon zest: from 1 lemon
- Lemon juice: 2 tbsp (30ml)
- Fresh dill: 2 tbsp, chopped
- Fresh parsley: 2 tbsp, chopped
- Garlic (minced): 2 cloves
- Salt and pepper: to taste

INSTRUCTIONS

1. In a bowl, mix olive oil, lemon zest, lemon juice, dill, parsley, garlic, salt, and pepper. Rub this mixture onto the salmon fillets.
2. Place salmon fillets in the air fryer basket.
3. Cook at 375°F (190°C) for 15 minutes.

Nutritional Value (per serving): Calories: 290, Total Fat: 17g, Carbohydrates: 1g, Protein: 30g

---

Air-Fryer Mediterranean Shrimp Salad

Preparation Time: 15 minutes
Cooking Time: 10 minutes

Servings: 4

INGREDIENTS

- Large shrimp (peeled and deveined): 1 lb (450g)
- Olive oil: 2 tbsp (30ml)
- Lemon juice: 1 tbsp (15ml)
- Cherry tomatoes: 1 cup, halved
- Cucumber: 1, diced
- Feta cheese: 1/2 cup, crumbled
- Fresh parsley: 1/4 cup, chopped
- Salt and pepper: to taste
- Mixed salad greens: 4 cups

INSTRUCTIONS

1. Toss shrimp in olive oil, lemon juice, salt, and pepper. Place in the air fryer basket.
2. Cook at 370°F (185°C) for 8-10 minutes, until shrimp are pink and opaque.
3. In a large bowl, mix cucumber, salad greens, feta, cherry tomatoes, and parsley. Top with cooked shrimp.

Nutritional Value (per serving): Calories: 230, Total Fat: 12g, Carbohydrates: 8g, Protein: 25g

Air-Fryer Tuna Patties with Olive Tapenade

Preparation Time: 20 minutes
Cooking Time: 12 minutes

Servings: 4

INGREDIENTS

- Canned tuna (drained): 2 cans (5 oz/140g each)
- Egg: 1
- Bread crumbs: 1/2 cup
- Olive tapenade: 2 tbsp
- Lemon zest: from 1 lemon
- Fresh parsley: 2 tbsp, chopped
- Olive oil: 1 tbsp (15ml)
- Salt and pepper: to taste

INSTRUCTIONS

1. In a bowl, combine tuna, egg, bread crumbs, tapenade, lemon zest, parsley, salt, and pepper. Form into 4 patties.
2. Brush patties with olive oil and place in the air fryer basket.
3. Cook at 375°F (190°C) for 12 minutes, turning once, until golden brown.

Nutritional Value (per serving): Calories: 210, Total Fat: 8g, Carbohydrates: 12g, Protein: 22g

---

Air-Fryer Zesty Herb Mussels

Preparation Time: 10 minutes
Cooking Time: 8 minutes

Servings: 4

INGREDIENTS

- Fresh mussels (cleaned and debearded): 2 lbs (900g)
- Olive oil: 2 tbsp (30ml)
- White wine: 1/4 cup (60ml)
- Fresh basil: 1/4 cup, chopped
- Fresh parsley: 1/4 cup, chopped
- Garlic (minced): 3 cloves
- Lemon juice: 1 tbsp (15ml)
- Salt and pepper: to taste

INSTRUCTIONS

1. In a bowl, mix olive oil, white wine, basil, parsley, garlic, lemon juice, salt, and pepper. Add mussels and toss to coat.
2. Transfer mussels to the air fryer basket.
3. Cook at 375°F (190°C) for 6-8 minutes, until mussels have opened, removing any that have not.

Nutritional Value (per serving): Calories: 220, Total Fat: 9g, Carbohydrates: 8g, Protein: 25g

Air-Fryer Garlic Lemon Scallops

Preparation Time: 10 minutes   **Servings: 4**
Cooking Time: 10 minutes

INGREDIENTS

- *Large scallops: 1 lb (450g)*
- *Olive oil: 2 tbsp (30ml)*
- *Garlic (minced): 3 cloves*
- *Lemon zest: from 1 lemon*
- *Fresh parsley: 1/4 cup, chopped*
- *Salt and pepper: to taste*

INSTRUCTIONS

1. Toss scallops in olive oil, garlic, lemon zest, parsley, salt, and pepper. Place scallops in the air fryer basket.
2. Cook at 375°F (190°C) for 10 minutes, turning once, until scallops are golden and opaque.

Nutritional Value (per serving): Calories: 210, Total Fat: 9g, Carbohydrates: 5g, Protein: 25g

---

Air-Fryer Crab-Stuffed Mushrooms

Preparation Time: 15 minutes   **Servings:** 4
Cooking Time: 12 minutes

INGREDIENTS

- *Large white mushrooms: 12, stems removed*
- *Crab meat (lump): 1 cup (225g)*
- *Cream cheese: 1/4 cup (60g)*
- *Green onions: 2, finely chopped*
- *Garlic (minced): 1 clove*
- *Lemon zest: from half a lemon*
- *Fresh parsley: 2 tbsp, chopped*
- *Olive oil: 1 tbsp (15ml)*
- *Salt and pepper: to taste*

INSTRUCTIONS

1. In a mixing bowl, combine crab meat, cream cheese, green onions, garlic, lemon zest, parsley, salt, and pepper.
2. Fill each mushroom cap halfway with the mixture.
3. Lightly brush the mushrooms' outside with olive oil. Place stuffed mushrooms in the air fryer basket.
4. Cook at 375°F (190°C) for 12 minutes or until filling is hot.

Nutritional Value (per serving): Calories: 160, Total Fat: 9g, Carbohydrates: 6g, Protein: 14g

Air-Fryer Mediterranean Calamari Rings

Preparation Time: 20 minutes (plus marinating time)

Cooking Time: 10 minutes
Servings: 4

INGREDIENTS

- *Fresh calamari tubes: 1 lb (450g), sliced into 1/2-inch rings*
- *Olive oil: 3 tbsp (45ml)*
- *Lemon juice: 2 tbsp (30ml)*
- *Garlic (minced): 2 cloves*
- *Fresh basil: 1/4 cup, chopped*
- *Salt and pepper: to taste*

INSTRUCTIONS

1. In a bowl, mix olive oil, lemon juice, garlic, basil, salt, and pepper. Add calamari rings, ensuring they're well-coated. Marinate for 1 hour.
2. Place marinated calamari rings in the air fryer basket in a single layer.
3. Cook at 400°F (205°C) for 10 minutes, turning once.

Nutritional Value (per serving): Calories: 190, Total Fat: 11g, Carbohydrates: 4g, Protein: 20g

---

Air-Fryer Spiced Tilapia with Tahini Drizzle

Preparation Time: 15 minutes
Cooking Time: 12 minutes

Servings: 4

INGREDIENTS

- *Tilapia fillets: 4 (6 oz/170g each)*
- *Olive oil: 2 tbsp (30ml)*
- *Paprika: 1 tsp*
- *Cumin: 1 tsp*
- *Tahini: 1/4 cup (60ml)*
- *Lemon juice: 1 tbsp (15ml)*
- *Fresh parsley: for garnish*
- *Salt and pepper: to taste*

INSTRUCTIONS

1. Brush tilapia fillets with olive oil. Sprinkle with paprika, cumin, salt, and pepper.
2. Place the fillets in the air fryer basket.
3. Cook at 375°F (190°C) for 12 minutes.
4. Mix tahini and lemon juice to create a drizzle. Pour over cooked tilapia and garnish with fresh parsley.

Nutritional Value (per serving): Calories: 265, Total Fat: 14g, Carbohydrates: 3g, Protein: 30g

Air-Fryer Herb-Crusted Cod

Preparation Time: 15 minutes
Cooking Time: 15 minutes

Servings: 4

INGREDIENTS

- Cod fillets: 4 (6 oz/170g each)
- Olive oil: 2 tbsp (30ml)
- Bread crumbs: 1/2 cup
- Fresh thyme: 2 tsp, chopped
- Fresh rosemary: 2 tsp, chopped
- Lemon zest: from 1 lemon
- Salt and pepper: to taste

INSTRUCTIONS

1. Mix bread crumbs, thyme, rosemary, lemon zest, salt, and pepper in a bowl.
2. Brush cod fillets with olive oil, then press each side into the bread crumb mixture.
3. Place the crusted fillets in the air fryer basket.
4. Cook at 375°F (190°C) for 15 minutes or until the fish is cooked through.

Nutritional Value (per serving): Calories: 220, Total Fat: 7g, Carbohydrates: 10g, Protein: 30g

Air-Fryer Shrimp with Garlic and Parsley

Preparation Time: 10 minutes
Cooking Time: 8 minutes

Servings: 4

INGREDIENTS

- Large shrimp (peeled and deveined): 1 lb (450g)
- Olive oil: 3 tbsp (45ml)
- Garlic (minced): 3 cloves
- Fresh parsley: 1/4 cup, chopped
- Lemon wedges: for serving
- Salt and pepper: to taste

INSTRUCTIONS

1. Toss shrimp in olive oil, garlic, parsley, salt, and pepper. Make sure each shrimp is well-coated.
2. Place shrimp in the air fryer basket in a single layer.
3. Cook at 400°F (205°C) for 8 minutes, turning once.
4. Serve with lemon wedges.

Nutritional Value (per serving): Calories: 240, Total Fat: 11g, Carbohydrates: 3g, Protein: 30g

Air Fryer Mediterranean Herbed Salmon

Preparation Time: 10 minutes
Cooking Time: 12 minutes

Servings: 2

INGREDIENTS

- 2 salmon fillets (6 oz each)
- 2 tbsp olive oil
- 1 tsp dried oregano
- 1 tsp dried thyme
- 1 garlic clove, minced
- Juice of 1 lemon
- Salt and pepper, to taste
- Lemon slices for garnish

INSTRUCTIONS

1. In a small bowl, mix together olive oil, oregano, thyme, garlic, lemon juice, salt, and pepper.
2. Brush the salmon fillets with the herb mixture.
3. Preheat the air fryer to 400°F (204°C).
4. Place the salmon in the air fryer basket, skin-side down.
5. Cook for 12 minutes.
6. Garnish with lemon slices and serve immediately.

Nutritional Value (per serving): Calories: 345, Fat: 23g, Carbohydrates: 2g, Protein: 34g

---

Air Fryer Garlic Shrimp with Feta

Preparation Time: 10 minutes
Cooking Time: 8 minutes

Servings: 4

INGREDIENTS

- 1 lb large shrimp, peeled and deveined
- 3 tbsp olive oil
- 3 garlic cloves, minced
- 1/2 tsp red pepper flakes
- 1/2 cup crumbled feta cheese
- 2 tbsp chopped parsley
- Salt and pepper, to taste
- Lemon wedges for serving

INSTRUCTIONS

1. In a bowl, toss shrimp with olive oil, garlic, red pepper flakes, salt, and pepper.
2. Preheat the air fryer to 380°F (193°C).
3. Place the shrimp in the air fryer basket in a single layer.
4. Cook for 4 minutes, then sprinkle feta cheese over the shrimp.
5. Continue cooking for another 4 minutes or until shrimp are pink and cooked through.
6. Serve with chopped parsley and lemon wedges.

Nutritional Value (per serving): Calories: 250, Fat: 15g, Carbohydrates: 2g, Protein: 26g

Air Fryer Mediterranean Stuffed Calamari

Preparation Time: 15 minutes
Cooking Time: 10 minutes

Servings: 2

INGREDIENTS

- 6 medium-sized calamari tubes, cleaned
- 1/2 cup cooked rice
- 1/4 cup chopped kalamata olives
- 1/4 cup chopped sun-dried tomatoes
- 2 tbsp capers
- 1 tbsp chopped parsley
- 1 garlic clove, minced
- Salt and pepper, to taste
- Olive oil spray

INSTRUCTIONS

1. In a bowl, mix together rice, olives, sun-dried tomatoes, capers, parsley, garlic, salt, and pepper.
2. Stuff each calamari tube with the rice mixture, securing the open end with a toothpick.
3. Preheat the air fryer to 370°F (188°C).
4. Spray the calamari and air fryer basket with olive oil.
5. Cook for 10 minutes, turning halfway, until calamari are tender.
6. Serve immediately.

Nutritional Value (per serving): Calories: 210, Fat: 7g, Carbohydrates: 22g, Protein: 15g

---

Air Fryer Lemon Pepper Cod

Preparation Time: 5 minutes
Cooking Time: 12 minutes

Servings: 4

INGREDIENTS

- 4 cod fillets (6 oz each)
- 2 tbsp olive oil
- 1 tbsp lemon pepper seasoning
- 1 lemon, juiced and zest
- Salt, to taste
- Lemon slices for garnish

INSTRUCTIONS

1. Drizzle cod fillets with olive oil and season with lemon pepper, lemon juice, zest, and salt.
2. Preheat the air fryer to 380°F (193°C).
3. Place the cod fillets in the air fryer basket.
4. Cook for 12 minutes or until cod is flaky and cooked through.
5. Garnish with lemon slices and serve immediately.

Nutritional Value (per serving): Calories: 190, Fat: 7g, Carbohydrates: 1g, Protein: 31g

Air Fryer Spiced Mussels

Preparation Time: 10 minutes   **Servings:** 2
Cooking Time: 6 minutes

INGREDIENTS

- 1 lb mussels, cleaned and debearded
- 1/4 cup white wine
- 1 tbsp olive oil
- 1 garlic clove, minced
- 1 tsp smoked paprika
- 1/4 tsp red pepper flakes
- 2 tbsp chopped parsley
- Salt and pepper, to taste
- Lemon wedges for serving

INSTRUCTIONS

1. In a bowl, mix together white wine, olive oil, garlic, smoked paprika, red pepper flakes, salt, and pepper.
2. Add mussels and toss to coat.
3. Preheat the air fryer to 370°F (188°C).
4. Place mussels in the air fryer basket.
5. Cook until mussels have opened (about 6 minutes).
6. Discard any mussels that did not open.
7. Serve with chopped parsley and lemon wedges.

Nutritional Value (per serving): Calories: 240, Fat: 10g, Carbohydrates: 10g, Protein: 25g

Chapter 8

Pasta

Air Fryer Mediterranean Penne with Cherry Tomatoes

Preparation Time: 10 minutes
Cooking Time: 15 minutes

Servings: 4

INGREDIENTS

- 2 cups penne pasta, cooked al dente
- 1 cup cherry tomatoes, halved
- 1/2 cup black olives, sliced
- 1/4 cup feta cheese, crumbled
- 2 tbsp olive oil
- 2 cloves garlic, minced
- 1 tsp dried basil
- Salt and pepper, to taste
- Fresh basil leaves for garnish

INSTRUCTIONS

1. In a bowl, combine cooked penne, cherry tomatoes, olives, feta cheese, olive oil, garlic, dried basil, salt, and pepper.
2. Preheat the air fryer to 350°F (177°C).
3. Transfer the pasta mixture to the air fryer basket.
4. Cook for 15 minutes, stirring halfway through, until tomatoes are soft and pasta is heated through.
5. Garnish with fresh basil leaves before serving.

Nutritional Value (per serving): Calories: 320, Fat: 12g, Carbohydrates: 45g, Protein: 10g

---

Air Fryer Spaghetti Squash Mediterranean Style

Preparation Time: 10 minutes
Cooking Time: 20 minutes

Servings: 2

INGREDIENTS

- 1 medium spaghetti squash, halved and seeds removed
- 2 tbsp olive oil
- 1/2 cup diced red bell pepper
- 1/4 cup diced onion
- 1/4 cup kalamata olives, sliced
- 1/4 cup crumbled feta cheese
- 2 tbsp chopped fresh parsley
- Salt and pepper, to taste

INSTRUCTIONS

1. Brush the inside of the spaghetti squash with olive oil and season with salt and pepper.
2. Preheat the air fryer to 370°F (188°C).
3. Lay the squash halves in the basket of the air fryer, cut side up.

4. Cook for 20 minutes or until the flesh is tender.
5. Scrape the squash strands into a bowl with a fork.
6. Mix in red bell pepper, onion, olives, feta cheese, and parsley.
7. Serve warm.

Nutritional Value (per serving): Calories: 290, Fat: 18g, Carbohydrates: 32g, Protein: 6g

---

Air Fryer Lemon Garlic Orzo with Spinach

Preparation Time: 5 minutes   **Servings:** 4
Cooking Time: 12 minutes

INGREDIENTS

- *2 cups orzo, cooked al dente*
- *2 tbsp olive oil*
- *2 cloves garlic, minced*
- *Zest and juice of 1 lemon*

- *1 cup baby spinach, chopped*
- *1/4 cup Parmesan cheese, grated*
- *Salt and pepper, to taste*
- *Lemon slices for garnish*

INSTRUCTIONS

1. In a bowl, combine cooked orzo, olive oil, garlic, lemon zest, lemon juice, spinach, Parmesan cheese, salt, and pepper.
2. Preheat the air fryer to 360°F (182°C).
3. Place the orzo mixture in the air fryer basket.
4. Cook for 12 minutes, stirring halfway through.
5. Garnish with lemon slices and serve warm.

Nutritional Value (per serving): Calories: 350, Fat: 10g, Carbohydrates: 53g, Protein: 13g

---

Air Fryer Mediterranean Mac and Cheese

Preparation Time: 10 minutes   **Servings:** 4
Cooking Time: 15 minutes

INGREDIENTS

- *2 cups elbow macaroni, cooked al dente*
- *1 cup milk*

- *1/2 cup crumbled feta cheese*
- *1/2 cup shredded mozzarella cheese*

- *1/4 cup sun-dried tomatoes, chopped*
- *1/4 cup chopped artichoke hearts*
- *2 tbsp chopped fresh basil*
- *Salt and pepper, to taste*

INSTRUCTIONS

1. In a bowl, mix together cooked macaroni, milk, feta cheese, mozzarella cheese, sun-dried tomatoes, artichokes, basil, salt, and pepper.
2. Preheat the air fryer to 360°F (182°C).
3. Transfer the macaroni mixture to the air fryer basket.
4. Cook for 15 minutes, stirring halfway through.
5. Serve warm.

Nutritional Value (per serving): Calories: 410, Fat: 15g, Carbohydrates: 53g, Protein: 18g

---

Air Fryer Pesto Zucchini Noodle Pasta

Preparation Time: 10 minutes
Cooking Time: 6 minutes

Servings: 2

INGREDIENTS

- *2 medium zucchinis, spiralized*
- *1/4 cup pesto sauce*
- *1/4 cup cherry tomatoes, halved*
- *2 tbsp pine nuts*
- *2 tbsp grated Parmesan cheese*
- *Salt and pepper, to taste*

INSTRUCTIONS

1. In a bowl, toss zucchini noodles with pesto sauce, cherry tomatoes, pine nuts, Parmesan cheese, salt, and pepper.
2. Preheat the air fryer to 360°F (182°C).
3. Place the zucchini noodle mixture in the air fryer basket.
4. Cook for 6 minutes, stirring halfway through, until noodles are tender.
5. Serve warm as a light and healthy pasta alternative.

Nutritional Value (per serving): Calories: 230, Fat: 18g, Carbohydrates: 12g, Protein: 7g

Air Fryer Tomato Basil Fusilli

Preparation Time: 5 minutes
Cooking Time: 10 minutes

Servings: 4

INGREDIENTS

- 2 cups fusilli pasta, cooked al dente
- 1 cup cherry tomatoes, halved
- 1/4 cup fresh basil, chopped
- 2 cloves garlic, minced
- 3 tbsp olive oil
- 1/4 cup grated Parmesan cheese
- Salt and pepper, to taste

INSTRUCTIONS

1. In a large bowl, combine cooked fusilli, cherry tomatoes, basil, garlic, olive oil, Parmesan cheese, salt, and pepper.
2. Preheat the air fryer to 360°F (182°C).
3. Transfer the pasta mixture to the air fryer basket.
4. Cook for 10 minutes, stirring halfway through, until the tomatoes are soft and the pasta is heated through.
5. Serve warm.

Nutritional Value (per serving): Calories: 320, Fat: 12g, Carbohydrates: 43g, Protein: 10g

---

Air Fryer Greek Pasta Salad

Preparation Time: 10 minutes

Servings: 4

INGREDIENTS

- 2 cups rotini pasta, cooked and cooled
- 1/2 cup cucumber, diced
- 1/2 cup cherry tomatoes, halved
- 1/4 cup red onion, thinly sliced
- 1/4 cup Kalamata olives, sliced
- 1/4 cup feta cheese, crumbled
- 3 tbsp olive oil
- 2 tbsp red wine vinegar
- 1 tsp dried oregano
- Salt and pepper, to taste

INSTRUCTIONS

1. In a large bowl, combine cooked rotini, cucumber, cherry tomatoes, red onion, olives, and feta cheese.
2. In a small bowl, whisk together red wine vinegar, olive oil, oregano, salt, and pepper.
3. Toss the spaghetti salad with the dressing to blend.
4. Refrigerate for at least 30 minutes before serving.

Nutritional Value (per serving): Calories: 320, Fat: 15g, Carbohydrates: 37g, Protein: 8g

Air Fryer Rigatoni with Spinach and Tomatoes

Preparation Time: 5 minutes
Cooking Time: 12 minutes

Servings: 4

INGREDIENTS

- *2 cups rigatoni pasta, cooked al dente*
- *1 cup fresh spinach, chopped*
- *1/2 cup cherry tomatoes, halved*
- *1/4 cup olive oil*
- *2 cloves garlic, minced*
- *Salt and pepper, to taste*
- *Grated Parmesan cheese, for serving*

INSTRUCTIONS

1. In a bowl, combine cooked rigatoni, spinach, cherry tomatoes, olive oil, and garlic. Season with salt and pepper.
2. Preheat the air fryer to 350°F (177°C).
3. Place the pasta mixture in the air fryer basket.
4. Cook for 12 minutes, stirring halfway through.
5. Serve warm, topped with grated Parmesan cheese.

Nutritional Value (per serving): Calories: 310, Fat: 14g, Carbohydrates: 38g, Protein: 8g

---

Air Fryer Lemon Artichoke Angel Hair

Preparation Time: 5 minutes
Cooking Time: 8 minutes

Servings: 4

INGREDIENTS

- *2 cups angel hair pasta, cooked al dente*
- *1/2 cup marinated artichoke hearts, chopped*
- *Zest and juice of 1 lemon*
- *2 tbsp olive oil*
- *2 tbsp capers*
- *Salt and pepper, to taste*
- *Fresh parsley, chopped for garnish*

INSTRUCTIONS

1. In a bowl, combine cooked angel hair, artichoke hearts, lemon zest, lemon juice, olive oil, and capers. Season with salt and pepper.
2. Preheat the air fryer to 360°F (182°C).
3. Transfer the pasta mixture to the air fryer basket.
4. Cook for 8 minutes, stirring halfway through, until heated through.
5. Serve warm, garnished with fresh parsley.

Nutritional Value (per serving): Calories: 280, Fat: 9g, Carbohydrates: 41g, Protein: 7g

Air Fryer Mediterranean Tortellini

Preparation Time: 5 minutes
Cooking Time: 8 minutes

Servings: 4

INGREDIENTS

- *2 cups cheese tortellini, cooked al dente*
- *1/4 cup sun-dried tomatoes, chopped*
- *1/4 cup black olives, sliced*
- *1/4 cup feta cheese, crumbled*
- *2 tbsp pesto sauce*
- *Salt and pepper, to taste*
- *Fresh basil leaves, for garnish*

INSTRUCTIONS

1. In a bowl, mix together cooked tortellini, sun-dried tomatoes, olives, feta cheese, and pesto sauce. Season with salt and pepper.
2. Preheat the air fryer to 360°F (182°C).
3. Transfer the tortellini mixture to the air fryer basket.
4. Cook for 8 minutes, stirring halfway through, until heated through.
5. Serve warm, garnished with fresh basil leaves.

Nutritional Value (per serving): Calories: 320, Fat: 15g, Carbohydrates: 35g, Protein: 12g

Chapter 9

Grains and Legumes

The nutritional prowess of grains and legumes doesn't end at mere sustenance. They are instrumental in combating modern-day malaises. The high fiber content ensures gut health, promoting digestion. The complex carbohydrates they offer ensure a slow release of energy, aiding in blood sugar control. Moreover, the plethora of minerals, vitamins, and antioxidants they bring to the table play a significant role in warding off chronic diseases.

What's truly magical, however, is how the Mediterranean cuisine elevates these basic staples into culinary masterpieces. The grains and legumes aren't just boiled and served; they're transformed. Infused with aromatic herbs, paired with fresh vegetables, or melded with rich sauces.

To truly embrace the Mediterranean diet, one must pay homage to its grains and legumes. For they are not mere side dishes or afterthoughts. They are the very foundation upon which the diet's reputation for health and taste stands. Rich in history, brimming with nutrients, and bursting with flavors, they remind us that sometimes, the most humble ingredients hold the key to the most profound culinary experiences.

In a world chasing superfoods and exotic ingredients, let's not forget the timeless wisdom of the Mediterranean: that good health, and great taste, often lies in the simple grains and legumes that have nourished civilizations for millennia.

Air-Fryer Lemon Quinoa & Chickpea Salad

Preparation Time: 15 minutes
Cooking Time: 20 minutes

Servings: 4

INGREDIENTS

- Quinoa: 1 cup (185g)
- Canned chickpeas: 1 cup (240ml), drained
- Fresh parsley: 1/4 cup (60ml), chopped
- Cherry tomatoes: 1 cup (240ml), halved
- Red onion: 1/4, finely chopped
- Lemon zest and juice: 1 lemon
- Olive oil: 2 tbsp (30ml)
- Feta cheese: 1/2 cup (120ml), crumbled
- Salt & pepper: to taste

INSTRUCTIONS

1. Cook quinoa according to package instructions.
2. In a bowl, toss chickpeas with 1 tbsp olive oil, salt, and pepper.
3. Place chickpeas in the air fryer basket and cook at 400°F (205°C) for 10 minutes, or until golden and crispy.
4. In a mixing bowl, combine cooked quinoa, air-fried chickpeas, parsley, tomatoes, and red onion.
5. Drizzle with remaining olive oil, lemon zest, lemon juice, salt, and pepper. Toss to combine.
6. Garnish with feta cheese before serving.

Nutritional Value (per serving): Calories: 320, Total Fat: 10g, Carbohydrates: 47g, Protein: 12g

---

Air-Fryer Mediterranean Barley Bowl

Preparation Time: 10 minutes
Cooking Time: 25 minutes

Servings: 4

INGREDIENTS

- Barley: 1 cup (200g)
- Red bell pepper: 1, diced
- Zucchini: 1, diced
- Olive oil: 2 tbsp (30ml)
- Garlic (minced): 2 cloves
- Fresh basil: 1/4 cup (60ml), chopped
- Salt & pepper: to taste
- Grated Parmesan: 1/4 cup (60ml)

INSTRUCTIONS

1. Cook barley according to package instructions.

2. In a bowl, toss diced red bell pepper and zucchini with minced garlic, salt, pepper, and olive oil.
3. Place vegetables in the air fryer basket and cook at 375°F (190°C) for 15 minutes, or until tender and slightly crispy.
4. In a mixing bowl, combine cooked barley with air-fried vegetables and fresh basil.
5. Serve warm, garnished with grated Parmesan.

Nutritional Value (per serving): Calories: 270, Total Fat: 7g, Carbohydrates: 45g, Protein: 8g

---

Air-Fryer Herb-Laced Lentil Cakes

Preparation Time: 20 minutes
Cooking Time: 15 minutes

Servings: 4

INGREDIENTS

- *Cooked lentils: 2 cups (480ml)*
- *Breadcrumbs: 1/2 cup (120ml)*
- *Egg: 1*

- *Fresh thyme & rosemary: 1 tbsp (15ml) each, chopped*
- *Salt & pepper: to taste*
- *Olive oil: for brushing*

INSTRUCTIONS

1. In a mixing bowl, mash lentils slightly, leaving some whole for texture.
2. Add breadcrumbs, egg, herbs, salt, and pepper. Mix until combined.
3. Form into 8 patties. Brush each patty lightly with olive oil.
4. Place in the air fryer basket and cook at 375°F (190°C) for 15 minutes, or until golden and crisp on the outside.

Nutritional Value (per serving): Calories: 220, Total Fat: 4g, Carbohydrates: 35g, Protein: 12g

---

Air-Fryer Farro & Vegetable Medley

Preparation Time: 10 minutes
Cooking Time: 25 minutes

Servings: 4

INGREDIENTS

- *Farro: 1 cup (200g)*

- *Assorted vegetables (like bell peppers, zucchini, cherry tomatoes): 2 cups (480ml), diced*

- *Olive oil: 2 tbsp (30ml)*
- *Fresh parsley: 1/4 cup (60ml), chopped*
- *Salt & pepper: to taste*
- *Crumbled goat cheese: 1/4 cup (60ml)*

INSTRUCTIONS

1. Cook farro according to package instructions.
2. Toss diced vegetables in olive oil, salt, and pepper.
3. Place in the air fryer basket and cook at 375°F (190°C) for 15 minutes.
4. Mix cooked farro with air-fried vegetables and fresh parsley.
5. Serve warm, topped with crumbled goat cheese.

Nutritional Value (per serving): Calories: 280, Total Fat: 8g, Carbohydrates: 46g, Protein: 9g

---

Air-Fryer Spiced Millet Cakes with Yogurt Dip

Preparation Time: 20 minutes
Cooking Time: 15 minutes

Servings: 4

INGREDIENTS

- *Millet: 1 cup (200g)*
- *Breadcrumbs: 1/3 cup (80ml)*
- *Egg: 1*
- *Cumin & paprika: 1/2 tsp (2.5ml) each*
- *Salt & pepper: to taste*
- *Olive oil: for brushing*
- *Greek yogurt: 1/2 cup (120ml)*
- *Fresh mint: 2 tbsp (30ml), chopped*

INSTRUCTIONS

1. Cook millet according to package instructions.
2. In a bowl, mix millet with breadcrumbs, egg, spices, salt, and pepper.
3. Form into patties and brush lightly with olive oil.
4. Air-fry at 375°F (190°C) for 15 minutes.
5. For the dip, mix yogurt with fresh mint. Serve alongside millet cakes.

Nutritional Value (per serving): Calories: 260, Total Fat: 5g, Carbohydrates: 43g, Protein: 10g

Air-Fryer Chickpea & Brown Rice Falafels

Preparation Time: 20 minutes
Cooking Time: 15 minutes

Servings: 4

INGREDIENTS

- *Cooked brown rice: 1 cup (200g)*
- *Canned chickpeas: 1 cup (240ml), drained*
- *Fresh parsley: 1/2 cup (120ml), chopped*
- *Garlic (minced): 2 cloves*
- *Cumin: 1 tsp (5ml)*
- *Salt & pepper: to taste*
- *Olive oil: for brushing*

INSTRUCTIONS

1. In a food processor, blend brown rice, chickpeas, parsley, garlic, cumin, salt, and pepper until you get a thick paste.
2. Form into small balls or patties. Brush each lightly with olive oil.
3. Air-fry at 375°F (190°C) for 15 minutes, or until golden brown.

Nutritional Value (per serving): Calories: 210, Total Fat: 3g, Carbohydrates: 41g, Protein: 7g

---

Air-Fryer Bulgur & Veggie Stuffed Peppers

Preparation Time: 20 minutes
Cooking Time: 20 minutes

Servings: 4

INGREDIENTS

- *Bell peppers (any color): 4, tops removed and seeded*
- *Bulgur: 1 cup (200g)*
- *Cherry tomatoes: 1 cup (240ml), halved*
- *Cucumber: 1, diced*
- *Olive oil: 2 tbsp (30ml)*
- *Lemon zest & juice: 1 lemon*
- *Fresh parsley: 1/4 cup (60ml), chopped*
- *Feta cheese: 1/2 cup (120ml), crumbled*
- *Salt & pepper: to taste*

INSTRUCTIONS

1. Cook bulgur according to package instructions.
2. In a mixing bowl, combine cooked bulgur, tomatoes, cucumber, olive oil, lemon zest, lemon juice, parsley, feta cheese, salt, and pepper.
3. Stuff each bell pepper halfway with the mixture.
4. Place peppers in the air fryer basket and cook at 375°F (190°C) for 20 minutes, or until peppers are tender.

Nutritional Value (per serving): Calories: 260, Total Fat: 8g, Carbohydrates: 42g, Protein: 8g

Air-Fryer Black Bean & Quinoa Bites

Preparation Time: 20 minutes
Cooking Time: 15 minutes

Servings: 4

INGREDIENTS

- *Cooked quinoa: 1 cup (185g)*
- *Black beans: 1 cup (240ml), drained and mashed*
- *Corn kernels: 1/2 cup (120ml)*
- *Cheddar cheese: 1/2 cup (120ml), grated*
- *Cumin & paprika: 1/2 tsp (2.5ml) each*
- *Salt & pepper: to taste*
- *Olive oil: for brushing*

INSTRUCTIONS

1. In a bowl, combine quinoa, mashed black beans, corn, cheese, cumin, paprika, salt, and pepper.
2. Form the mixture into small patties. Brush each patty lightly with olive oil.
3. Air-fry at 375°F (190°C) for 15 minutes, or until golden and crisp.

Nutritional Value (per serving): Calories: 280, Total Fat: 8g, Carbohydrates: 42g, Protein: 12g

---

Air-Fryer Herbed Couscous Cakes

Preparation Time: 15 minutes
Cooking Time: 15 minutes

Servings: 4

INGREDIENTS

- *Cooked couscous: 2 cups (370g)*
- *Fresh herbs (like parsley, dill, chives): 1/2 cup (120ml), chopped*
- *Egg: 1*
- *Salt & pepper: to taste*
- *Olive oil: for brushing*

INSTRUCTIONS

1. In a bowl, mix couscous, fresh herbs, egg, salt, and pepper.
2. Shape into patties and brush them with olive oil.
3. Air-fry at 375°F (190°C) for 15 minutes.

Nutritional Value (per serving): Calories: 200, Total Fat: 4g, Carbohydrates: 36g, Protein: 7g

---

Air-Fryer Mediterranean Lentil Patties

Preparation Time: 20 minutes
Cooking Time: 15 minutes

Servings: 4

INGREDIENTS

- *Cooked lentils: 1 cup (200g)*
- *Bread crumbs: 1/2 cup (120ml)*
- *Egg: 1*
- *Fresh cilantro: 1/4 cup (60ml), chopped*

- *Garlic (minced): 2 cloves*
- *Cumin: 1 tsp (5ml)*
- *Salt & pepper: to taste*
- *Olive oil: for brushing*

INSTRUCTIONS

1. In a bowl, combine lentils, breadcrumbs, egg, cilantro, garlic, cumin, salt, and pepper.
2. Form into patties, then brush them with olive oil.
3. Air-fry at 375°F (190°C) for 15 minutes.

Nutritional Value (per serving): Calories: 230, Total Fat: 4g, Carbohydrates: 38g, Protein: 11g

Chapter 10

Desserts

Air-Fryer Olive Oil & Citrus Cake0

Preparation Time: 15 minutes
Cooking Time: 25 minutes

Servings: 6

INGREDIENTS

- *Olive oil: 1/2 cup (120ml)*
- *Sugar: 3/4 cup (150g)*
- *Eggs: 3*
- *Flour: 1 1/2 cups (180g)*

- *Baking powder: 2 tsp (10ml)*
- *Lemon zest: from 1 lemon*
- *Orange zest: from 1 orange*
- *Salt: a pinch*

INSTRUCTIONS

1. In a bowl, whisk together olive oil, sugar, and eggs until creamy.
2. Gradually add in the flour, lemon zest, orange zest, baking powder, and salt. Mix until smooth.
3. Transfer batter to a greased air fryer-safe baking pan.
4. Air-fry at 320°F (160°C) for 25 minutes, or insert a toothpick. If it is ready, it should come out clean.

Nutritional Value (per serving): Calories: 330, Total Fat: 15g, Carbohydrates: 44g, Protein: 5g

---

Air-Fryer Almond & Honey Bites

Preparation Time: 20 minutes
Cooking Time: 12 minutes

Servings: 8

INGREDIENTS

- *Ground almonds: 1 1/2 cups (140g)*
- *Honey: 1/2 cup (120ml)*
- *Egg white: from 1 egg*

- *Vanilla extract: 1 tsp (5ml)*
- *Salt: a pinch*

INSTRUCTIONS

1. In a bowl, combine all ingredients and mix until you achieve a sticky consistency.
2. Shape mixture into small balls.
3. Air-fry at 350°F (175°C) for 12 minutes, or until golden.

Nutritional Value (per serving): Calories: 200, Total Fat: 10g, Carbohydrates: 26g, Protein: 5g

Air-Fryer Date & Walnut Bars

Preparation Time: 15 minutes
Cooking Time: 20 minutes

Servings: 8

INGREDIENTS

- Dates (pitted and chopped): 1 cup (175g)
- Walnuts (chopped): 1/2 cup (60g)
- Flour: 1 cup (120g)
- Brown sugar: 1/2 cup (100g)
- Butter (melted): 1/4 cup (60ml)

- Eggs: 2
- Vanilla extract: 1 tsp (5ml)
- Baking powder: 1 tsp (5ml)
- Salt: a pinch

INSTRUCTIONS

1. In a bowl, mix flour, brown sugar, melted butter, eggs, vanilla, baking powder, and salt.
2. Fold in dates and walnuts.
3. Spread mixture in a greased, air fryer-safe pan.
4. Air-fry at 340°F (170°C) for 20 minutes, or insert a toothpick. If it is ready, it should come out clean.

Nutritional Value (per serving): Calories: 280, Total Fat: 12g, Carbohydrates: 40g, Protein: 5g

---

Air-Fryer Lemon & Lavender Shortbread

Preparation Time: 20 minutes
Cooking Time: 12 minutes

Servings: 8

INGREDIENTS

- Flour: 1 1/2 cups (180g)
- Sugar: 1/2 cup (100g)
- Butter (cold and cubed): 1/2 cup (115g)

- Lemon zest: from 1 lemon
- Dried lavender flowers: 1 tsp (5ml)
- Salt: a pinch

INSTRUCTIONS

1. In a food processor, combine all ingredients and pulse until dough forms.
2. Roll out dough and cut into desired shapes.
3. Air-fry at 330°F (165°C) for 12 minutes.

Nutritional Value (per serving): Calories: 250, Total Fat: 12g, Carbohydrates: 34g, Protein: 3g

Air-Fryer Chocolate & Olive Oil Muffins

Preparation Time: 15 minutes
Cooking Time: 18 minutes

Servings: 6

INGREDIENTS

- Olive oil: 1/4 cup (60ml)
- Sugar: 1/2 cup (100g)
- Eggs: 2
- Flour: 1 cup (120g)
- Unsweetened cocoa powder: 1/4 cup (25g)
- Baking powder: 1 tsp (5ml)
- Salt: a pinch
- Semi-sweet chocolate chips: 1/4 cup

INSTRUCTIONS

1. In a bowl, whisk together olive oil, sugar, and eggs.
2. Gradually add flour, cocoa powder, baking powder, salt, and chocolate chips. Mix until combined.
3. Divide batter among air fryer-safe muffin cups.
4. Air-fry at 350°F (175°C) for 18 minutes, or insert a toothpick. If it is ready, it should come out clean.

Nutritional Value (per serving): Calories: 290, Total Fat: 14g, Carbohydrates: 38g, Protein: 5g

---

Air-Fryer Fig & Honey Tartlets

Preparation Time: 20 minutes
Cooking Time: 15 minutes

Servings: 6

INGREDIENTS

- Fresh figs (quartered): 12
- Honey: 1/3 cup (80ml)
- Pie crust dough: 1 sheet
- Cream cheese: 1/2 cup (115g)
- Lemon zest: from 1 lemon

INSTRUCTIONS

1. Roll out the pie crust dough and cut into circles to fit into tartlet molds.
2. Fill each tartlet with a spoonful of cream cheese.
3. Place two fig quarters onto each tartlet.
4. Drizzle with honey and sprinkle with lemon zest.
5. Air-fry at 340°F (170°C) for 15 minutes.

Nutritional Value (per serving): Calories: 265, Total Fat: 12g, Carbohydrates: 36g, Protein: 4g

Air-Fryer Almond & Cinnamon Cookies

Preparation Time: 15 minutes   **Servings:** 10
Cooking Time: 10 minutes

INGREDIENTS

- *Ground almonds: 1 1/2 cups (140g)*
- *Sugar: 1/2 cup (100g)*
- *Cinnamon: 2 tsp (10ml)*
- *Egg white: from 1 egg*

INSTRUCTIONS

1. Mix ground almonds, sugar, cinnamon, and egg white until you get a consistent mixture.
2. Shape into small cookies.
3. Air-fry at 350°F (175°C) for 10 minutes.

Nutritional Value (per serving): Calories: 135, Total Fat: 8g, Carbohydrates: 14g, Protein: 4g

---

Air-Fryer Coconut & Orange Slices

Preparation Time: 20 minutes   **Servings:** 8
Cooking Time: 12 minutes

INGREDIENTS

- *Desiccated coconut: 1 cup (85g)*
- *Orange zest: from 2 oranges*
- *Sugar: 1/2 cup (100g)*
- *Eggs: 2*

INSTRUCTIONS

1. Combine all ingredients in a mixing bowl until well incorporated.
2. Shape the mixture into small slices.
3. Air-fry at 340°F (170°C) for 12 minutes, or until golden.

Nutritional Value (per serving): Calories: 115, Total Fat: 6g, Carbohydrates: 13g, Protein: 3g

Air-Fryer Pistachio & Chocolate Clusters

Preparation Time: 10 minutes
Cooking Time: 5 minutes

Servings: 8

INGREDIENTS

- *Dark chocolate (melted): 1/2 cup (90g)*
- *Pistachios (shelled and coarsely chopped): 1/2 cup (60g)*

INSTRUCTIONS

1. Mix the melted chocolate with the chopped pistachios.
2. Form little clusters using spoonfuls of the mixture on parchment paper.
3. Place the parchment paper in the air fryer basket.
4. Air-fry at 300°F (150°C) for 5 minutes.
5. Let them cool before serving.

Nutritional Value (per serving): Calories: 105, Total Fat: 7g, Carbohydrates: 9g, Protein: 3g

---

Air-Fryer Rose & Berry Cheesecake Bites

Preparation Time: 25 minutes
Cooking Time: 15 minutes

Servings: 8

INGREDIENTS

- *Cream cheese: 1 cup (230g)*
- *Sugar: 1/2 cup (100g)*
- *Mixed berries (like raspberries, blueberries, blackberries): 1/2 cup (70g)*
- *Rose water: 1 tsp (5ml)*
- *Egg: 1*
- *Graham cracker crumbs: 1/2 cup (60g)*

INSTRUCTIONS

1. In a bowl, blend cream cheese, sugar, egg, and rose water until smooth.
2. Gently fold in the mixed berries.
3. Spoon the mixture into air fryer-safe molds, pressing down a layer of graham cracker crumbs at the base.
4. Air-fry at 320°F (160°C) for 15 minutes, or until set.

Nutritional Value (per serving): Calories: 210, Total Fat: 11g, Carbohydrates: 24g, Protein: 4g

Chapter 11

28-Day Meal Plan

This meal plan is a template and should be adjusted according to individual nutritional needs and preferences.

Tips for Your Meal Plan:

1. **Portion Control:** Adapt portion sizes to your personal dietary needs.

2. **Stay Hydrated:** Drink as much water as possible throughout the day.

3. **Adjust as Needed:** Feel free to swap out ingredients based on dietary needs and availability.

4. **Moderation with Desserts:** While desserts are part of the plan, they should be enjoyed in moderation. Desserts are designed to be enjoyed occasionally. You can choose to have them every day or just a few times a week, depending on your dietary preferences.

5. **Snacks:** For snacks, you can rotate between different options each day. Include fresh fruits, nuts, and other Mediterranean-friendly choices like Greek yogurt or cheese with whole-grain crackers.

6. **Incorporate Physical Activity:** Complement your diet with regular physical activity, as is typical in Mediterranean lifestyles.

7. **Balanced Nutrition:** Each meal is balanced to provide a proper amount of protein, vegetables, and healthy fats.

Week 1

Day	Breakfast	Snack	Lunch	Dinner	Dessert
1	Air Fryer Mediterranean Frittata	Air-Fried Stuffed Olives	Mediterranean Herb-Infused Chicken Wings + Garlic & Lemon Broccoli Florets	Lemon-Oregano Chicken Thighs + Air-Fried Mediterranean Asparagus	Air-Fryer Olive Oil & Citrus Cake
2	Air Fryer Greek Yogurt Pancakes	Mediterranean Veggie Chips	Air Fryer Mediterranean Turkey Patties + Mediterranean Roasted Red Peppers	Air-Fryer Lemon-Herb Salmon Fillets + Crispy Mediterranean Brussels Sprouts	Air-Fryer Almond & Honey Bites
3	Air Fryer Mediterranean Breakfast Sandwich	Feta-Stuffed Mini Bell Peppers	Air-Fryer Greek Lemon Chicken Drumsticks + Air Fryer Eggplant Rounds	Air-Fryer Tuna Patties with Olive Tapenade + Mediterranean Potato Wedges	Air-Fryer Date & Walnut Bars
4	Air Fryer Olive & Tomato Shakshuka	Mediterranean Air-Fried Falafel	Mediterranean Stuffed Chicken Breasts + Crispy Mediterranean Zucchini Fritters	Air-Fryer Spiced Tilapia with Tahini Drizzle + Stuffed Mediterranean Bell Peppers	Air-Fryer Lemon & Lavender Shortbread
5	Air Fryer Mediterranean Veggie Omelette	Air-Fried Bruschetta Bites	Air-Fryer Chicken Shawarma Wraps + Mediterranean Beet Fries	Air-Fryer Garlic Lemon Scallops + Air Fryer Mediterranean Cauliflower Steaks	Air-Fryer Chocolate & Olive Oil Muffins
6	Air Fryer Herbed Mediterranean Potatoes	Air-Fried Greek Meatballs (Keftedes)	Air-Fryer Mediterranean Herb Chicken Skewers + Garlic & Lemon Broccoli Florets	Air-Fryer Mediterranean Beef Kebabs + Air-Fried Mediterranean Asparagus	Air-Fryer Fig & Honey Tartlets
7	Air Fryer Mediterranean Breakfast Wraps	Air-Fried Spinach and Cheese Triangles	Air-Fryer Chicken Meatballs with Feta and Spinach + Crispy Mediterranean Brussels Sprouts	Air-Fryer Mediterranean Spiced Chicken Legs + Mediterranean Potato Wedges	Air-Fryer Almond & Cinnamon Cookies

Week 2

Day	Breakfast	Snack	Lunch	Dinner	Dessert
8	Air Fryer Mediterranean Avocado and Egg Toast	Mediterranean Hummus Cups	Air-Fryer Mediterranean Lamb Chops + Air-Fried Mediterranean Cauliflower Steaks	Air-Fryer Herb-Crusted Pork Tenderloin + Crispy Mediterranean Zucchini Fritters	Air-Fryer Coconut & Orange Slices
9	Air Fryer Mediterranean Veggie and Feta Scramble	Air-Fried Mediterranean Quesadillas	Air-Fryer Lemon-Herb Salmon Fillets + Stuffed Mediterranean Bell Peppers	Air-Fryer Mediterranean Beef Skewers + Mediterranean Roasted Red Peppers	Air-Fryer Pistachio & Chocolate Clusters
10	Air Fryer Mediterranean Stuffed Avocados	Air-Fried Mediterranean Stuffed Mushrooms	Air-Fryer Rosemary-Infused Beef Sliders + Mediterranean Beet Fries	Air-Fryer Shrimp with Garlic and Parsley + Air Fryer Eggplant Rounds	Air-Fryer Rose & Berry Cheesecake Bites
11	Air Fryer Mediterranean Sweet Potato Hash	Air-Fried Olive Tapenade Crostini	Air-Fryer Mediterranean Steak Fajitas + Air-Fried Mediterranean Asparagus	Air Fryer Mediterranean Tortellini	Air-Fryer Olive Oil & Citrus Cake
12	Air Fryer Lemon-Garlic Asparagus	Mediterranean Zucchini Fritters	Air-Fryer Mediterranean Herb-Infused Chicken Wings + Garlic & Lemon Broccoli Florets	Air-Fryer Mediterranean Shrimp Salad + Air-Fried Mediterranean Cauliflower Steaks	Air-Fryer Almond & Honey Bites
13	Air Fryer Mediterranean Breakfast Bruschetta	Air-Fried Mediterranean Stuffed Peppers	Air Fryer Mediterranean Penne with Cherry Tomatoes	Air Fryer Lemon Pepper Cod + Crispy Mediterranean Brussels Sprouts	Air-Fryer Date & Walnut Bars
14	Air Fryer Zucchini and Feta Fritters	Air-Fried Greek Meatballs (Keftedes)	Air-Fryer Garlic Lemon Scallops + Mediterranean Potato Wedges	Air-Fryer Mediterranean Beef and Veggie Platter	Air-Fryer Lemon & Lavender Shortbread

Week 3

Day	Breakfast	Snack	Lunch	Dinner	Dessert
15	Air Fryer Mediterranean Avocado Toast	Air-Fried Bruschetta Bites	Air-Fryer Spiced Tilapia with Tahini Drizzle + Mediterranean Beet Fries	Air-Fryer Mediterranean Spiced Chicken Legs + Air-Fried Mediterranean Cauliflower Steaks	Air-Fryer Chocolate & Olive Oil Muffins
16	Air Fryer Mediterranean Breakfast Burrito	Mediterranean Veggie Chips	Air-Fryer Herb-Crusted Cod + Garlic & Lemon Broccoli Florets	Air-Fryer Chicken Shawarma Wraps + Air Fryer Eggplant Rounds	Air-Fryer Almond & Cinnamon Cookies
17	Air Fryer Mediterranean Chia Seed Pudding	Air-Fried Mediterranean Quesadillas	Air Fryer Spaghetti Squash Mediterranean Style + Crispy Mediterranean Zucchini Fritters	Air-Fryer Mediterranean Lamb Chops + Mediterranean Roasted Red Peppers	Air-Fryer Fig & Honey Tartlets
18	Air Fryer Mediterranean Quinoa Breakfast Bowl	Air-Fried Spinach and Cheese Triangles	Air-Fryer Beef and Veggie Mediterranean Platter	Air-Fryer Lemon-Herb Salmon Fillets + Air-Fried Mediterranean Asparagus	Air-Fryer Coconut & Orange Slices
19	Air Fryer Mediterranean Breakfast Wraps	Air-Fried Olive Tapenade Crostini	Air-Fryer Mediterranean Beef Skewers + Crispy Mediterranean Brussels Sprouts	Air-Fryer Tuna Patties with Olive Tapenade + Mediterranean Potato Wedges	Air-Fryer Pistachio & Chocolate Clusters
20	Air Fryer Mediterranean Spinach and Egg Scramble	Air-Fried Mediterranean Stuffed Mushrooms	Air-Fryer Rosemary-Infused Beef Sliders + Garlic & Lemon Broccoli Florets	Air-Fryer Garlic Lemon Scallops + Mediterranean Roasted Red Peppers	Air-Fryer Rose & Berry Cheesecake Bites
21	Air Fryer Toasted Mediterranean Avocado Toast	Air-Fried Greek Meatballs (Keftedes)	Air Fryer Lemon Artichoke Angel Hair	Air-Fryer Mediterranean Shrimp Salad	Air-Fryer Olive Oil & Citrus Cake

Week 4

Day	Breakfast	Snack	Lunch	Dinner	Dessert
22	Air Fryer Mediterranean Frittata	Mediterranean Hummus Cups	Air-Fryer Chicken Meatballs with Feta and Spinach	Air-Fryer Mediterranean Beef Kebabs + Mediterranean Roasted Red Peppers	Air-Fryer Date & Walnut Bars
23	Air Fryer Olive & Tomato Shakshuka	Air-Fried Bruschetta Bites	Air-Fryer Mediterranean Turkey Patties with Garlic + Lemon Broccoli Florets	Air-Fryer Shrimp with Garlic and Parsley + Air-Fried Mediterranean Cauliflower Steaks	Air-Fryer Lemon & Lavender Shortbread
24	Air Fryer Mediterranean Veggie Omelette	Air-Fried Spinach and Cheese Triangles	Air-Fryer Herb-Crusted Pork Tenderloin + Crispy Mediterranean Brussels Sprouts	Air-Fryer Mediterranean Spiced Chicken Legs + Mediterranean Potato Wedges	Air-Fryer Chocolate & Olive Oil Muffins
25	Air Fryer Herbed Mediterranean Potatoes	Air-Fried Mediterranean Stuffed Mushrooms	Air Fryer Spaghetti Squash Mediterranean Style + Air Fryer Mediterranean Cauliflower Steaks	Air-Fryer Tuna Patties with Olive Tapenade + Air-Fryer Mediterranean Stuffed Peppers	Air-Fryer Almond & Cinnamon Cookies
26	Air Fryer Mediterranean Breakfast Wraps	Air-Fried Mediterranean Quesadillas	Air-Fryer Mediterranean Beef Skewers + Mediterranean Beet Fries	Air-Fryer Lemon-Herb Salmon Fillets + Air-Fried Mediterranean Asparagus	Air-Fryer Fig & Honey Tartlets
27	Air Fryer Mediterranean Avocado and Egg Toast	Air-Fried Greek Meatballs (Keftedes)	Air Fryer Lemon Artichoke Angel Hair	Air-Fryer Mediterranean Herb Chicken Skewers + Air Fryer Eggplant Rounds	Air-Fryer Coconut & Orange Slices
28	Air Fryer Mediterranean Veggie and Feta Scramble	Air-Fried Olive Tapenade Crostini	Air-Fryer Rosemary-Infused Beef Sliders + Crispy Mediterranean Zucchini Fritters	Air-Fryer Garlic Lemon Scallops with Garlic + Lemon Broccoli Florets	Air-Fryer Pistachio & Chocolate Clusters

Appendix

Conversion Tables

COOKING CONVERSION CHART

WEIGHT

IMPERIAL	METRIC
1/2 oz	15 g
1 oz	29 g
2 oz	57 g
3 oz	85 g
4 oz	113 g
5 oz	141 g
6 oz	170 g
8 oz	227 g
10 oz	283 g
12 oz	340 g
13 oz	369 g
14 oz	397 g
15 oz	425 g
1 lb	453 g

TEMPERATURE

FAHRENHEIT	CELSIUS
100 °F	37 °C
150 °F	65 °C
200 °F	93 °C
250 °F	121 °C
300 °F	150 °C
325 °F	160 °C
350 °F	180 °C
375 °F	190 °C
400 °F	200 °C
425 °F	220 °C
450 °F	230 °C
500 °F	260 °C
525 °F	274 °C
550 °F	288 °C

MEASUREMENT

CUP	ONCES	MILLILITERS	TBSP
8 cup	64 oz	1895 ml	128
6 cup	48 oz	1420 ml	96
5 cup	40 oz	1180 ml	80
4 cup	32 oz	960 ml	64
2 cup	16 oz	500 ml	32
1 cup	8 oz	250 ml	16
3/4 cup	6 oz	177 ml	12
2/3 cup	5 oz	158 ml	11
1/2 cup	4 oz	118 ml	8
3/8 cup	3 oz	90 ml	6
1/3 cup	2.5 oz	79 ml	5.5
1/4 cup	2 oz	59 ml	4
1/8 cup	1 oz	30 ml	3
1/16 cup	1/2 oz	15 ml	1

Index

Made in the USA
Las Vegas, NV
20 February 2024